CRIME-VICTIM STORIES

CRIME-VICTIM STORIES

New York City's Urban Folklore

ELEANOR WACHS

INDIANA
UNIVERSITY
PRESS
Bloomington and Indianapolis

Manufactured in the United States of America

Library of Congress Cataloging-in-Publication Data

Wachs, Eleanor F.
Crime-victim stories.

Bibliography: p.
Includes index.
1. Victims of crimes—New York (N.Y.)   2. Urban
folklore—New York (N.Y.)   I. Title.
HV6250.3.U53N488   1988   398'.355   87-46243
ISBN 0-253-31494-1
ISBN 0-253-20491-7 (pbk.)

1 2 3 4 5   92 91 90 89 88

CONTENTS

For My Parents,
Tillie Wachs
and in memory of my father,
Frank Wachs

Acknowledgments

Crime-Victim Stories: New York City's Urban Folklore is a collaborative effort: folklorists depend on their informants to willingly share their personal experiences. In an attempt to investigate the victim experience as part of the folklore of the city world, I interviewed many New Yorkers who consented to participate in this collaboration. I am grateful to them.

My appreciation is extended to several institutions that helped support my research: Indiana University, for a doctoral grant for one of my earliest forays into the field in 1977; the library staff at Brown University, where I was a visiting assistant professor during several rewriting stages of the manuscript (1979–1981); and the University of Massachusetts-Boston, which provided me with two research grants for fieldwork and research (1983, 1984).

I also want to express my appreciation to the many people who unknowingly supported my research, particularly the helpful staffs of the Grand Army Plaza Library, Brooklyn, New York, and the Mid-Manhattan Library of the New York Public Library, especially the Periodicals Division staff of both institutions.

In the course of this work, I have received the support and guidance of many friends and colleagues. For reading the manuscript and supplying helpful criticism, I should like to thank Linda Morley. For reading sections of the manuscript, for offering suggestions, and for other kindnesses, I should like to thank Aviva Hay, Ellen Nylen, Mary Ellen Brown, Annelen Archbold, Camilla Collins, Brunhilde Biebuyck, Simon J. Bronner, and Jan Harold Brunvand. I am grateful to my friends for their constant support and encouragement, especially my dear friend Paula Cohen, and Ruth Bobrow, Elizabeth Cooke Stevens, Lesley T. Sharpe, and Joan Brittain. Members of the New York City Chapter of the New York Folklore Society were helpful in their suggestions and comments, especially Barbro Klein, Barbara Kirshenblatt-Gimblett, and Lee Haring. My colleagues at the University of Massachusetts-Boston offered constructive criticism and support, especially Edwin Gittleman, Frederick Danker, Pamela J. Annas, Norma Kroll, and particularly Lois P. Rudnick.

My greatest debt is to the late Richard Dorson, the doyen of folklore studies in the nation until his death in 1981. His renewed interest in urban folklore toward the end of his life, and his encouragement and support of my work as a graduate student at the Folklore Institute, Indiana University, and later as a colleague, were appreciated then, as they are today.

Introduction

Thirteen-year-old Bernadette raced home from school on a chilly autumn afternoon across the busy Brooklyn streets. She knew that she would find her mother with her cronies at a neighbor's apartment, sitting and drinking around a table covered with nearly empty liquor bottles. Bernadette greeted her mother, got from her the key to their own heavily locked apartment, ran back home, changed her clothes, and was ready to join her friends in the building backyard. But first, she needed to return the key to her mother in the adjacent building. Instead of waiting for the elevator, she decided to take the stairs, two at a time, up to the sixth floor. She never made it.

I was raped at thirteen. You didn't know that? This is what happened. When I was thirteen, November 13, 1962, I lived at 417 Maple Street, fourteenth floor. My mother was drinking very heavily at that time. My mother was hanging around with these drinking buddies at 414 across the street. So I had to do something: I had to go home. I picked up the key from my mother at 414. I went home, changed my clothes, did whatever I had to do, and was on my way back. It was getting late; I decided to walk up the stairs to the sixth floor. There were only six floors. So I ran up, and as I was putting my hand on the stairway door to open it, to go into the hallway where all the apartments were, when this voice from behind me said, "DON'T TOUCH THAT DOOR!" So of course you're taught to obey authority, right? So I just froze. And he put a knife to my throat. A butcher knife, like, with a blade about that long [approximately ten inches]. And he said, "If anybody comes, don't say anything," right? So we walked up to the top floor, which was above the roof landing. And then we walked to the other side, because it had two landings. Then I took off all my clothes. And all this and, uhm, [pause] he had his fun. . . . I *knew,* and even now I still know, that he didn't want to hurt me. He wanted sex, and that was it. But I was the third victim. Well, I know one of the girls he attacked before. A girl named Loretta. And then he had tried to attack another woman, but she screamed and she scared him away. So I was the third victim. So what happened was, when he was really getting into what he was doing, his hands were in my hair and all that. He had put down the knife. And that's when I grabbed it. I just grabbed the first thing, and I grabbed the blade. And I grabbed it with both hands.

> And he started to try to pull it away. And he tried to kick me, and I started to
> scream. . . .[1]

In a Manhattan delicatessen during a busy midday hour in June, 1976,
Bernadette Potter, a heavyset twenty-eight-year-old black woman, told me
her crime-victim story. Although the incident had happened fifteen years
earlier, her voice quivered and her hands moved wildly as she spoke. I
noticed her curled fingers, and a long, meandering scar on her left hand.
The scar is a reminder of Bernadette's struggle with the rapist, as she
grabbed his knife by the blade and slashed his heel, marking him for
capture by the police minutes after the rape.

At the restaurant, office workers and shoppers wolfed down sand-
wiches, gulped down coffee, and shared loud conversations with other
customers and waiters. In this common urban setting, our conversation
lasted nearly three hours. We were two native New Yorkers, friends for
years, catching up on news and talking about life in the city. Despite
having worked together in an office years before, and our resulting friend-
ship, I had not known until that afternoon that Bernadette had been raped.
Like many New Yorkers to whom I would speak about urban crime during
the next four years, Bernadette told me one story after another:

> This happened to a distant cousin of mine. This is *really weird*. They had
> moved into a building, and the son was fifteen years old. He met these two
> guys who befriended him. You live in the neighborhood, so why not?
> Something like a month later, these two guys knocked on the door, and of
> course, the woman . . . the mother . . . came in. . . . They ripped her off,
> tried to kill them, killed the mother. They took her son, slashed him several
> times, and hung him upside down in the closet for him to die. That's sick,
> yes?[2]

Bernadette told her stories in a straightforward, dramatic style, sprinkling
them with traces of wit and sarcasm. It is a style of narrative performance
used by many New Yorkers to tell these gruesome tales of city life. This
type of story is often embedded into conversations and is a part of the
city's oral tradition.

These stories about crime victimization would prompt folklorists to
explore those aspects of urban existence that pertain to an urban folklore:
the customs and traditions indigenous to city life. Urban folklore involves
a pattern of responses between people that depends on a shared set of
culturally determined traits, assumptions, and expectations. These traits
reflect the well-known characteristics of this world: population density,
heterogeneity, alienation, anonymity, bystander apathy, and invasion of
privacy, among others. These are the traits common to these stories.[3] The
following account is typical:

> I was going to a concert in the city with my friends and saw this guy being
> mugged, but we didn't stop. We would have been late for the concert. I can't
> say that. But we didn't stop, and that's the truth. I don't know if we would
> have stopped if we hadn't been late or that's just a good excuse. Maybe we
> wouldn't have stopped. Just a guy getting beat up on the street corner. But
> it's kind of scary to stop and help when there are so many people who are
> armed.[4]

One of the most popular traditions among New Yorkers is telling stories
about significant events in their daily lives. The specific content of these
urban tales may vary, but they often share common characteristics and
themes. Many New Yorkers, for example, recount their experiences with
power blackouts, transit or garbage strikes, battles at traffic court, or
eccentric characters. As storytellers, they select their accounts from an
extensive repertory of narratives that includes other stories, perhaps more
personal or intimate. Yet, whether intimate or commonplace, many of
these tales deal with some aspect of crime vicitimization or some feature
of urban life:

> A friend of mine bought a newspaper one evening. And as he was walking
> home—as he was just ready to come into the house—there were a few boys
> waiting in the lobby. He didn't see them. But once he got into the elevator,
> they pounced on him. And they beat him up very badly. They didn't want
> anything. They just wanted to beat him up.(**M-11**)[5]

Everyone has such stories to tell, whether about crime-victim situations,
urban foul-ups, or some other, equally dramatic, aspect of city life.

Today, most folklorists agree that the scope and content of their field of
study are the traditional materials transmitted either by oral face-to-face
interaction, such as sharing a joke, or in a partially verbal or nonverbal
way, as when a master craftsperson teaches an apprentice a traditional
skill. These products of human creativity (jokes, family stories, folk songs,
quilts, etc.) appear in patterned recurrent forms, which are always in flux
because of the nature of oral transmission. The recurrence of form and the
variation within the replicated form of a traditional item are two characteristic qualities of folklore. Understanding how folklore functions within
a culture is an important concern of the folklorist, as is the relationship
between these products of human interaction and the people who create,
perform, use, and pass them on to others.[6] Regardless of the environment
in which it flourishes, rural or urban, folklore reflects its cultural milieu.
Thereby, it serves as an effective data base for research and analysis.

To earlier folklorists who studied mainly rural communities, tradition
often meant those expressive materials or documents appearing in culture
that were passed on transgenerationally; that is, from father to son or
mother to daughter. This "tradition," they claimed, had to pass the "test of

time." Folktales survived because they engendered significant cultural values, and as such were "carried on" or "passed down" like family heirlooms. This limited view of folklore transmission has given way to a larger, more complex picture. It has been fully demonstrated, for example, that traditions are constantly supplanted and that mass media and technology actively create and disseminate both old and new traditions. Through the media, news is received almost as soon as it occurs. And almost as quickly, listeners fashion impressions, thoughts, and stories about these events.[7] In our technological age, one criterion in the former traditional process of transmitting folklore—that is, "the test of time"— has been eroded. At the same time, the media have become a significant force in the rapid dissemination of folklore.

Folklorists do not assign greater value to studying one folk culture or form of lore over another. Though they may often disagree as to appropriate theoretical approaches, such differences merely reflect the healthy vitality of the discipline. Contemporary folklorists do agree, however, that they study the role of tradition in culture. As this study makes clear, my interest lies in a specific tradition of the urban world—the crime-victim narrative.

Folklore offers explanations and solutions that serve as a mediating force for some of humankind's most difficult dilemmas. In fact, today's folklorist would claim that the traditional folk wisdom embodied in lore offers solutions to cultural enigmas, or provides vehicles that folk groups can use to reflect upon, rationalize, or solve everyday problems. As an important body of knowledge used for stockpiling traditional solutions to common problems, folklore "provides guidelines for behavior" and creates mechanisms by which the group can psychologically handle the unexpected once it happens.[8] Crime-victim stories include such mechanisms.

One out of every three Americans has had some experience with crime victimization.[9] Americans in general have become increasingly fearful of crime in their homes, neighborhoods, and cities. Few venture casually into the streets after dark; many stay home regardless of the hour. Others will not leave for vacation before they have stored their money in the refrigerator, put valuable jewelry in a safe-deposit box, or made sure the daily newspapers do not pile up outside the door. Sometimes these methods do not work:

> My apartment was robbed . . . when I was in Puerto Rico having a good time. . . . And my neighbor was keeping an eye out, and my neighbors were informed as well. And P.S. they came in through the fire escape. I got a message at the place I was staying. It was a guest house. My sister was pregnant at the time. So, I said if she had the baby to let me know. Well, P.S. there was a message, "By the way, your apartment was robbed."[10]

During 1977, when I started conducting the fieldwork for this study, nationwide crime-victim statistics were shocking. The Uniform Crime Report for 1977 reported that a murder took place every twenty-seven minutes in the United States. A forcible and violent rape occurred every eight seconds. Someone was robbed every seventy-eight seconds, or burglarized every ten seconds; there was a larceny-theft every five seconds. Most astonishing, one aggravated assault occurred each minute.[11] Stephen Schaefer, in his book *The Victim and His Criminal,* notes that, as impressive as these statistics are, they do not present an accurate nationwide picture of the crime victim's situation. "Official crime statistics," he writes, "seem unable to cope with the difficulties of drawing an accurate picture of the amount of crime and the number of criminals; and victim statistics to the extent that they present a numerical analysis of crime and criminals are sources of error, and even less reliable knowledge is obtainable if they concern the victim."[12] Statistics, then, seem to be neither accurate nor reliable in providing a clear picture about crime victimization: it is in their stories that victims' voices are heard.

> What happens? Either I'm carrying a pocketbook or they come up and snatch a pocketbook and keep on running. Some of them are on bicycles. So, you're gonna run after them on a bicycle? You can't do it! There's so much crime in the city! What's the point of calling the cops?[13]

Our society is undergoing a change in how people regard the criminal-justice system. Many of the senior citizens I spoke to, like the one who gave the above commentary, view the justice system as an impersonal bureaucracy. They claim that juvenile offenders who commit "adult" crimes plea bargain with the help of their court-appointed lawyers; they are quickly released and then return to the streets to commit more crimes. The often-heard saying that "a judge is liberal until he is mugged" reflects the notion that the criminal-justice system is becoming increasingly lenient because prisons are dangerously overcrowded. The "Miranda" decision, which assures offenders' civil rights, has had a widespread impact, affecting not only the arrest methods of the police but also the public's attitude toward crime. Many people I spoke with believed that the crime victim, unlike the criminal, has few if any rights, or even any sound recourse to compensation and restitution. This attitude prevails despite the fact that several states have passed victims'-rights legislation.[14]

In this confuson, victims and their families and friends often resort to the "traditional" activity of storytelling to cope with the persistent problem of urban crime. In general, Americans are fearful of violent crime; by talking about it and telling stories to one another, victims are able to express this common fear.

The urban lifestyle breeds alienation, as sociologist Louis Wirth and others detailed decades ago.[15] No longer do neighbors watch out for neighbors. Good Samaritans are exceptional. The rare do-gooder is the one who makes the evening headlines, hailed as an instant folk hero. Another traditional feature of city life is bystander apathy, as exemplified in the 1964 murder of Kitty Genovese. In this widely publicized incident, neighbors watched and listened to the woman's cries for help as she was brutally stabbed outside the door of her Queens apartment. No one offered aid.[16] A rising crime rate, fear for one's own safety, and lack of concern for the welfare of others are the byproducts of our urban crime-infested lives.

Like most New Yorkers, I had often thought about crime and how my awareness of it affected my daily experiences. The horror of the Kitty Genovese affair had affected many New Yorkers, me among them. Most wondered why no one came to her rescue.

In 1977, when I began collecting the majority of the crime-victim stories presented here, David Berkowitz, the "Son of Sam," was stalking several neighborhoods, mostly in Queens, searching for the dark-haired women he would soon murder. He was the talk of the town. But the dramatic events concerning the "Son of Sam" were not the only ones spoken about. Informants told of street muggings, local store holdups, apartment break-ins, and more. Unlike the unusual Berkowitz case, which captured the city's attention for several months, these crimes that I heard about were everyday events.[17] It was this ordinary element of the narrative that appealed to me as a subject of research, rather than the bizarre mass murderer.

As a folklorist, I was intrigued by the urban oral tradition of crime-victim stories. I became interested in how people talk about crime-victim events and what they imply when they do. The more I became aware of their prominence, the more I became fascinated by the world view story-tellers would project when relating these tales. How often did Bernadette tell of her escape on the roof? What did her story reveal about city life and its dangers? Was her story idiosyncratic? Did others have similar stories to share, and would they follow similar or different patterns? Thinking about these questions, I narrowed my focus to four concerns: (1) How do urbanites, New Yorkers in this case, fashion reports about the social reality of crime and crime victimization? (2) How do these stories relate to other narratives common to folklore? (3) How do these stories incorporate urban folkways? and (4) How do these stories reflect the world view of the urban community?

An important area of investigation lay in the apparent traditions inherent in the attitudes and behavior of the victims. Why did the New Yorkers I spoke with find life there so attractive despite the high occurrence of crime within their workplaces and neighborhoods? Why were they willing to tolerate the city's high cost of living, the polluted environment, the failed transportation system, the increases in street crime? City life offers an abundance of goods and services, cultural events, exotic restaurants, multicultural neighborhoods, and a variety of groups and diversity of peoples. Many of the people I spoke with insisted upon calling New York City the "capital of the country." The crime-victim stories they related supplied some of the answers.

I purposely distinguish the crime-victim narrative from the crime narrative. My informants, as crime victims, provided stories with the victim as hero/heroine, or as a character related in a third-person account. Crime victims were usually presented as central to the action. A few stories were rehashed newspaper accounts, but rarely was the offender featured as the main character. According to studies, the crime stories recounted by offenders focus on the crime itself; the victims are outside the offenders' range of thought and concern. The difference between offender and victim lore, then, is significant. It neatly parallels the difference in content between crime-victim stories and crime stories.[18] Crime-victim narratives are stylized and structured formulaic stories that recapitulate incidents between a victim and an offender. The crime narrative describes an event about the offender, who is often the storyteller. For example, an incarcerated criminal's boasting about a successful "hit," or a prisoner's recounting of exploits outside of the prison would qualify as crime narratives but not as crime-victim narratives.

The following narrative exemplifies the differences between the two types of stories. A young man had just stopped off at the dry cleaner's. He had his receipt, name and address included, pinned onto his garment. In an impulsive moment on the way home, he broke into an apartment and helped himself to the owner's possessions. Since he left his ticketed garment behind, he was quickly arrested. This brief narrative is representative of the crime story. The victim—as person—is insignificant. He or she is just a means to an end, an instrument for obtaining the goods or money the offender demands, or a convenient object for the criminal's hostility or rage. Little, if any, moralizing appears in the crime narrative. In the crime-victim narrative, however, the narrator often empathizes with the victim's plight, and narrators and audience are relieved when an account includes the possibility that the offender might be apprehended.

By the end of the first stage of my fieldwork (1976–1977), I had reached many tentative conclusions that would shape subsequent observations (1979, 1981, 1984, 1985). I found that informants who recounted their crime-related experiences did not categorize crimes or use labels to distinguish different types of crimes. They merely told one story of victimization after another. Many times in their stories, they included generalizations about crime and city life. For example, one woman related an incident that had occurred in her apartment building. She interlaced her narrative with personal opinions concerning the victim, the owning of jewelry, and the urbanite's fear of crime:

> There was an incident here during the summer in Building Three. There was a man. He was a widower. He was in his seventies. He was an antiques dealer. Evidently his neighbors knew that his apartment was a very expensive apartment. How it happened I don't really know. But one day, the neighbors saw that his door was off its hinges. So when they went to investigate, they found the man bloodied on the floor, and he was completely robbed of all the antiques. . . . They never found out who did it. . . . You just have to keep quiet if you have any valuables. And you're very foolish if you keep valuables in the house, because in this day and age you just can't advertise what you've got. You don't wear what you have, and it's very unfortunate, because you wear jewelry out of sentimental value and certainly for pleasure. But . . . what's the sense of buying beautiful things . . . if you can't enjoy them? Or if you invite people into your home to enjoy it with you? You're afraid to invite them in for fear of who's gonna tell the next one what you have. It's a very bad situation.[19]

Initially, I suspected that the street mugging story would be the modern counterpart to the nineteenth-century tall tale, filled with boasts and exaggerations. "How big was that bear?" would be replaced with "Yeah, you were mugged? How big was the knife?" I expected that the details of the crime-victim incident would become aggrandized, embellished, and more fantastic at each retelling. I anticipated that the tall tale of American folklore had evolved into the new and unbelievable story of the urban street.

After fieldwork in the winter of 1976, my hypothesis changed. In selecting only the mugging story as a subtype of crime-victim lore, I had overlooked a variety of other experiences that city dwellers were eager to share. "No, I wasn't mugged"—a common reply to my question about this type of incident—frequently was followed by the further comment, "but I've been robbed!" Although the dramatic stories about crime victims eventually surpassed my earlier expectations, not all informants touched on the areas I finally chose to collect: mugging, rape, and murder. The street mugging story remained the largest and richest category for collecting. As my data base increased, the mugging-story-as-tall-tale hypothesis fell apart. The stories were not fabrications of events but were, rather, realistic, straightforward accounts. I collected over 150 narratives, 120 of which are included in the Appendix.

For convenience, I have divided the narratives into the following general categories: the mugging story (**M**); the murder story (**MR**); and the rape story (**R**). In addition, each is numbered sequentially; a letter/number designation follows each narrative embodied in the discussion that follows. Thus, **M-9** refers to the ninth mugging story in the Appendix.

Conducting fieldwork involves making contacts with people, establishing rapport, and conducting interviews. Much of the work that a fieldworker does takes place after the interview, when tapes are transcribed word for word, field notes are recorded, and the material is reviewed. I collected the crime-victim stories by tape-recording interviews, and I often used an interview guide, kept in view during the sessions, to make certain that major topics were discussed. The interview guide was connected to the major goals of my interest: the collection of crime-related incidents narrated as true accounts, and a discussion of the effects of the incidents—in particular, the protective behavioral changes my informants made as a result of being victimized or of having heard accounts of such incidents. I interviewed fifty people and talked with many others. While I transcribed all interviews, I present here only a portion of the narratives and commentary of my informants. I draw, as well, on notations from my fieldwork journal.

The city dweller's cognitive map determined my selection of informants. Each urbanite has a complex mental image of the city world, the neighborhoods, the subway system, and even the best routes to take crosstown. All informants were familiar with the centrally located areas of Manhattan, and knew their neighborhoods well.[20] Many people I spoke with had little knowledge of other boroughs or other neighborhoods. For example, some Brooklynites knew little of the Bronx, and stated they had never been there despite its relative proximity. Recognizing that some boundary had to be established, and because of my own knowledge of Brooklyn and Manhattan, I spoke mostly with residents of those areas.

A technique of conducting fieldwork, including urban fieldwork, is to establish bridges between people, who then lead to others they assume will be helpful. In seeking informants, I needed to discover the crime-victim network. Lines of association began to develop through contacts with friends, relatives, and acquaintances, many of whom did direct me to additional informants. A network began to develop. I met informants in groups or through group associations. For example, through the aid of a social worker employed by a Brooklyn agency devoted to serving the elderly, I volunteered my time to organize a couple of weekly discussion groups. Crime was a daily reality to these people, since they lived in a high-crime area and were constantly fearful of being victimized or already had been victimized. They often talked about their experiences. The social worker told me the following story about one of the agency's clients:

A client who I knew very well . . . was raped and killed right on Ocean Avenue and Church [Avenue]. Oh, such a lovely lady. . . . Little lady, very frail. . . . Maybe weighed ninety pounds. . . . She would do anything for anyone. And this guy followed her into her apartment. He tied her up. He raped and he killed her. He bashed her head in. . . . You know what I think about when I think of her? How scared she must have been. . . .[21]

The group-discussion format served an important function: it gave the victims an opportunity to share their experiences with a sympathetic audience to whom they could vent their anger. I was a willing listener.

Others began to hear about me, and I became known as the person interested in "crime stuff." Informants frequently introduced me by this description to their friends, who in turn had their own stories to tell. Often, I met them in their homes, after working hours, or during lunch hours near their workplaces. Many interviews took place in coffee shops, and before too long I knew the ones with the most conducive atmosphere for collecting.

Informants were not particularly difficult to secure. As in most fieldwork, some serendipitous experiences occurred. For example, one afternoon I was waiting to interview a woman whom I had met at a party some weeks earlier. We planned to rendezvous in the lobby of a large university building in Manhattan, and then to go to a nearby coffee shop for our interview. While waiting for her, I began to chat with a middle-aged man who was sitting next to me on a bench. Before long, I found out he was a college professor. He was quick to tell me several of his urban horror escapades. One story he told included being held up at gunpoint on the subway.

Informants differed in racial and ethnic background, occupation, and social class, reflecting the cultural diversity of New York City. The majority were middle- or lower-middle-class. Three-fourths of the informants were college-educated. I spoke with office workers, salespeople, actors, schoolteachers, college students, nurses, and many others. Crime victimization seems to be a great leveler. I was concerned here not with which groups were more victimized than others, but with how informants captured their experiences and told them as stories about urban life.

As expected, a majority of informants questioned me about the purpose of my research. When I replied that I was interested in the urban folkways of New York City, and said that crime and victimization played a significant role in the city's oral tradition, they seemed puzzled. Of course, to many of my informants, folklore was something difficult to identify or to explain; many thought it was not a part of their daily lives. This is a common fieldwork experience for folklorists.

As I became involved in gathering these narratives, I became increasingly more interested in women informants, because they were so open in their discussions. For example, rape, a subject which was more or less taboo a few years earlier, was now being discussed. Recent cultural changes brought about by the women's movement have substantially increased the accessibility of such formerly suppressed personal experiences. (Bernadette's rape story is one such example.)[22] During the period of this investigation, the influence of the women's movement became widespread. Women's rape and crisis centers opened. Consciousness-raising centers and women's self-defense courses became common, especially in New York City. Susan Brownmiller's groundbreaking feminist study about rape, *Against Our Will,* published in 1975, made its impact.[23] This increased awareness of women's issues made it inevitable that these stories would surface. And they did.

In studying New Yorkers, I was on familiar ground. The knowledge of my home terrain made working in the city easier for me than for someone new to the area. I made my way through the city streets and the complex transporation system to each fieldwork appointment without difficulty; yet, I could never anticipate an interview's outcome. People I spoke with shared personal experiences that for some had produced severe emotional scars. Some New Yorkers I interviewed had recently been crime victims and were still suffering from the aftershock. Some became emotionally upset when describing the details of their experience. Others expressed outrage. The discussion of intimate details and the expression of strong emotion demanded strict confidentiality, and each individual was assured of his or her anonymity. In this study, I have given all informants pseudonyms appropriate to their personalities, particular interests, or ethnic backgrounds.

By listening to these crime-victim experiences almost daily for several months, I started to understand the anxiety and vulnerability my informants expressed. After hearing about one woman's return home one night, I wondered what I would do if faced with the same situation:

> My friend Emily was robbed at knifepoint. She saw these black guys. They were a few blocks away from her house. They were about eighteen. They looked suspicious to her. She was a little afraid, but she passed them, and they didn't look as though they were following her. So she figured it was just her imagination. Then when she got to her house, as she goes and as she presses the elevator [button] and she gets in there, and the door opens rather than remaining closed to go up. And these guys are right outside the elevator. And she was right! There was something to worry about. And they took out a knife. And they asked for money. So she gave them her money. (M-3)[24]

Fortunately, I did not share Emily's fate. People continually asked me whether I had been victimized, but I had no incidents to report to them.

After a promise of confidentiality and an explanation of my intentions, most informants seemed enthusiastic about my work and flattered to contribute to the study. However, some became anxious, even distraught, when telling their stories. A lull in the conversation, lasting from a few brief seconds to a few minutes, always punctuated the telling. It became clear that each person needed some restorative psychological space during the sensitive moments of the interview. They, as tellers, needed to regain self-control. They expressed this need through their silence. Sometimes during the liveliest of discussions, informants became quiet, passive, reflective. Watching their expressions, I sat with them and waited. I assumed that they were recalling the crime scenes just narrated to me. Usually, after a few moments, we went on with the interview; but if someone was unusually distraught, he or she became withdrawn after the anticipated silence. I either dropped the topic at that point or returned to it later, when my informant seemed more composed. If necessary, I would quickly complete the interview. Only once did an informant request terminating an interview. In general, I found the people I spoke with willing to share their crime-victim stories with me, and I appreciated their efforts.

CRIME-VICTIM STORIES

CHAPTER ONE

An Urban Storytelling Session

On a rainy Sunday afternoon in March 1978, a talkative cabbie in a black-and-yellow taxi jammed on his brakes, screeched to a stop, and dropped me off on the corner near Clara Gold's home. I had come to Clara's to record the crime-victim stories I anticipated would be exchanged during a get-together of her friends, a group of New York professional women. I expected that these women, like most New Yorkers, would tell personal-experience narratives to one another. Their conversations would likely revolve around a familiar and traditional topic of city folklore: urban crime.

In New York City folk culture, the subject of crime and the experiences of crime victims and potential victims are often used as conversational icebreakers, invitations for humorous exchange, or a means to transmit street smarts. Crime-victim experiences are transmitted in these three ways at social gatherings, as well as in a variety of other common urban places: standing in line at a bank or a department store, chatting with fellow passengers on the subways, sharing a table in a crowded restaurant, talking at a party. Such experiences are so common, and a topic of conversation so popular, that even strangers feel at ease revealing to one another the details of victimization. In Clara's living room, the women spontaneously shared crime-victim narratives for several hours on a weekend afternoon. Their enjoyable social event is illustrative of the way that many New Yorkers talk about these incidents.

The particular setting for this story-swapping session was a Brooklyn apartment on Park Slope. A group of New York City women were meeting for an afternoon tea. All were college-educated and middle-class. They met as members of a literary club and shared a love for mystery fiction. During the course of this Sunday afternoon, they discussed several common concerns of New Yorkers: crime, law and order, politics, cultural happenings, and neighborhood events. But a large portion of the discussion was devoted to exchanging crime-victim stories.

1

Like many literary-interest groups, this one was devoted to the fiction of Arthur Conan Doyle. Eight members of the group were present during the afternoon: four turned out to be narrators of crime-victim stories; four served as the audience. The women met periodically throughout the year, and several socialized outside of the group on a regular basis. As a result, a few friendships had developed and matured.[1]

Just because the women were interested in Holmes, one cannot presume that they had a fascination with urban crime events, as well. A distinction must be made between Arthur Conan Doyle's fictional accounts of notorious criminals and mysterious events, and the victimizations of day-to-day life in New York City nearly one hundred years later. One can attribute an appreciation for the stories about Sherlock Holmes to a fascination for nineteenth-century London and the trappings of the socially ordered Victorian world. The New York City stories reveal, instead, a world of chaos and unexplainable violence. The crime-victim stories were discussed separately from the group's Sherlockian business affairs. That this group had a particular interest in detective fiction is a coincidence. Other groups of New Yorkers, just as well educated or from similar economic backgrounds, also incorporate crime-victim stories into their social conversations.

As already mentioned, four women at the event were prominent tellers of crime-victim stories. Irene Whitefield, the organizer of the group and coordinator of its activities, was a native New Yorker in her twenties living in the Chelsea district of Manhattan, a recently gentrified neighborhood. Irene was employed as a secretary and pursued her acting interests by appearing in off-off-Broadway theater. She was a flamboyant storyteller, perhaps because of her acting ability. Karen Green was a native New Yorker living on Manhattan's Upper East Side. Married, in her thirties, she was a registered nurse in one of the city's largest hospitals. She was loquacious and dramatic in her delivery of stories, and she obviously enjoyed the group's attention when she shared her city experiences. Pamela Day, originally from a small town in Massachusetts, had moved to New York City after graduating from a large university upstate. Pam was in her mid-twenties, lived on Manhattan's Upper West Side, and had continued to study as a geologist despite difficulty in finding employment. Clara Gold was a personnel administrator in her late twenties. She was a Brooklynite and was host of the gathering.

The four others in the group played an important role in the swapping of the crime-victim stories. Audience members are not silent partners. They enhance the narrator's rendition by offering validating comments, expressing sympathy for the character/victim within the story, and urging the narrators to continue by expressing appreciative and laudatory comments such as, "Oh, that's a good one!" or "That's funny."

During the afternoon, fourteen stories were presented: ten were specifically crime-related, while the other four related to common types of victimization. Broken down by subject, they told of one murder, four muggings, and five robberies and burglaries. The remaining accounts functioned as frames for subsequent stories or as lengthy introductory sequences, setting the stage for what might be seen as a narrative competition. Two remaining stories, one about a shopping-bag lady and the other about a shopping-bag man, presented two common urban characters that often appear in these stories. Additional characters include the victim, the offender, the apathetic bystander, and the ill-tempered subway or bus rider. With the exception of the victim, offender, and witness, none of the other characters are personalized; each is a stock character of the urban scene. They serve as the dramatis personae for these stories, and their actions are presented without explanation, since they are all well-known figures of the city's streets.

The crime-victim stories the women related were included in a conversation that went on with few interruptions for approximately three hours. Occasionally, the conversation was stopped momentarily by members' leaving the living room and walking into the adjoining dining room for refreshments. The women felt free to enter and leave the conversation at will. As the afternoon wore on and as the guests became more relaxed, narratives were exchanged at an increasing rate, and few interruptions occurred. The beginning of these narrative exchanges could be considered conversational icebreakers. Since the members had not recently seen each other, the stories served as a way to open up communication between them. They each could identify with a familiar form of activity: talking about crime.

The session began with a story about a handicapped person, a victim not of crime but of society. Like the crime-victim story, the story about the handicapped person is told as if it is part of a comedian's slapstick routine. Why the women laughed at the handicapped person's predicament is hard to tell, though there is a parallel here with a type of folk narrative, the urban legend. (By definition, an urban legend is a story about an extraordinary event, told for truth, and attributed to an ambiguous source.) The legend is about an injured man and an ambulance driver. Upon hearing how the patient became injured, the ambulance driver laughed so hard he dropped the stretcher, causing the man further injury. In the case of this afternoon session, the first story functioned in the same way as the legend.[2] Though it is not a crime-victim story per se, it is an "urban" story, and the apathetic bystander character, in this case, is a policeman. Ann Holland, the story's narrator, was a woman in her mid-thirties who worked as an editor in a large publishing house in New York City. Her Woody Allen-like tale of urban frustration began the round of storytelling. Ann then became a member of the audience and told only one other story during the rest of the afternoon.

Ann started by introducing her story, saying: "It's a really terrible story, it's sorta sick." She giggled nervously and pushed her glasses up over her small nose and fidgeted with her short, thick hair. She sounded a bit tentative, almost apologetic, as she began talking, tugging at the hem of her skirt and pulling it down over her chubby knees.

She told about an incident that had happened a month before the tea. She and a friend were caught in a traffic jam behind a large oil truck that was making a delivery to a house on an icy, hilly street. A yellow car in front of Ann's had pulled out and attempted to go around the truck. She had moved her car right behind it, and expected to wait until the delivery of oil was completed. Though two lane, the street was quite narrow. Suddenly, a Cadillac came up over the rise of the hill and was just about to collide with the yellow car that had pulled out beside the truck. With typical urban etiquette, the Caddy driver wouldn't budge to let the yellow car pass. "Suddenly, a police car pulled up behind us," Ann said dramatically. "And he's gonna control everything!" Ann bellowed powerfully, imitating the policeman: "*YOU* GO DOWN THAT STREET, AND *YOU* COME DOWN HERE!" He commanded the drivers of the yellow car and the Caddy to go in opposite directions, but his plan was stalemated. Suddenly, the Caddy driver opened his car door and began yelling at the top of his lungs. "He's sure screaming about something," Ann said. "And, I look around the corner, and I see the wheelchair." The yellow car drove around the tanker, and the Cadillac crept slowly down the hill. "So sure enough, behind this Cadillac is this guy in a wheelchair in the middle of the street. . . . You could see the chains on the wheelchair to take it up the hill." Then the man fell out of the wheelchair, and as he lay prostrate on the icy street, the chair wheels started to spin around. Then she caught her breath and continued. "And the guy is lying there. THE GUY IS LYING THERE ON THE STREET!" Ann howled. Her indignation was directed at the policeman, who stared for a few seconds at the paralyzed man floundering on the pavement, then went back to his squad car and drove off. "I mean, the guy doesn't have a license [laughter], and the cop looks at the guy, and I guess he determined that the guy was not dead, and that since he was not driving a motor vehicle it was not the cop's concern . . . he wasn't a crossing guard. . . . So he got back into his car and drove off!"

The group members, intent on hearing Ann's conclusion to the story, let out squeals of shock and surprise, disappointed by the policeman's show of apathy. But she resolved her story: "So about five guys from the neighborhood came running out. They hoisted him up in the chair and pushed him off! And we drove down the street falling over with laughter."

Ann confided to the women that she had told the above story to several friends at the publishing house. "It's really sick! The poor guy in the wheelchair . . . flipping over the wheels," she said hysterically. But Ann continued almost immediately with another short story about another handicapped person and a confrontation with a policeman.

Once the laughter subsided, Karen Green, sitting next to Ann, presented her own story about another urban character type—the cabbie. Karen described a recent spill on the ice and a temporary handicap of her own. She had fallen into a pothole on a city street after stepping off a bus, twisted her ankle, and required medical attention. With her husband, she hailed a cab for a dash to a nearby emergency room. "The cab driver must have thought that I was in labor, because he started racing through the traffic, 'Goddamn traffic! Goddamn traffic! Wouldn't cha know it! Just when you gotta get to a hospital in a hurry!'" At this point in her story, Karen switched from a serious to a humorous tone. Since the women were sitting in a cozy circle, she could glance around at them; she smiled and in a very pleasant and calm voice said, "I say to the cabbie, 'What's the big hurry? . . . I ain't gonna *die yet*!'" as she continued her story. The audience trusted Karen's judgment about the seriousness of her accident, since she was a nurse at a major metropolitan hospital and faced emergency situations daily.

Pam Day, a taffy-haired willowy woman, had been sitting across from Ann and Karen. She broke into the conversation and started to tell of her own escapade with a familiar urban character—the ill-mannered transportation rider. Her delivery was fast-paced, different from her usual cool, reserved, unruffled style.

Pam told of an accident on a mid-Manhattan bus. "I've heard a one-liner that I will probably never hear again in my life," she said. The story was about a blind man who was on a half-empty bus and found himself ahead of two men; all three were trying to get off at the Port of Authority stop. Suddenly realizing that the terminal was in view, a woman passenger from the back of the bus charged toward the front door. She pushed past the two men and started elbowing the blind man, shouting, "OUTTA MY WAY! OUTTA MY WAY! THIS IS MY STOP!" Everyone on the bus was shocked by the woman's outburst. Then someone said sarcastically, "Lady, he's blind." The woman's response: "I don't care if he is blind, he should look where he's going!"

Victimization and physical disability was the central theme in the above narratives. Yet in each of the three stories, the narrators used humor: to comment on urban aggression, as a way to make light of their own and others' misfortunes, and to distance themselves from the trauma of the experience. At the tea party, humor was used in several common ways. For example, people often laugh at others' frailties, at embarrassing situations (such as Karen's spill), or at a lack of social grace (such as the woman on the bus exhibited).[3] When Karen mentioned that she had fallen into the pothole, Clara Gold remarked, "What are you goin' to do? Send a case of them to the mayor?" The women roared with laughter.[4]

The conversation could have been followed by a discussion about the problems of the handicapped in society. Instead, the tone changed when Clara jumped in, and in a shrill voice told her first story of the afternoon: "Listen to this. I've got one better." She began:

> Some woman is standing on the train station. It was like two o'clock in the morning, and she's waiting at Forty-second Street or Fifty-ninth Street, or something like that. There were three people on the station. Someone goes over to lean over the platform and look, and she steps on another woman's foot, right? And this woman whose foot she stepped on started screaming and said to her, "You know, when the train comes, I'm gonna push you in front of it." And when the train came, she pushed her in front of it! I would be out on the street in thirty seconds. But I mean, it's the kind of thing that if someone said to me, "Lady, I'm gonna push you in front of the train," I would say, "Thank you. Sorry." Kiss her foot and then, you know, *not* be hangin' around. **(MR-14)**

One of the aims of the narrator of a crime-victim story is to shock the audience, and Clara did just that. While the dramatic style in which these stories are narrated is important for their telling, their illustrative, didactic intent is paramount. Clara's story highlights the unpredictable consequences of urban living for the everyday citizen. What is so frightening is the precariousness of someone's life in such a common setting. Yet, that is exactly the point. The ordinary setting and the extraordinary event that takes place within the story frame not only lend believability to the story but also insure its shock value. In the narrative above, the victim is suddenly thrust into a life-threatening situation.

After Clara's story, Karen Green commented by saying, "I heard about that happening during the rush hour. I read it in the newspaper that it was rush hour. And that was the one where the train was coming out of the tunnel, and the lights were seen. The woman pushed the first woman on the track, and the woman went running up the tracks, and somebody at the far end helped to pull her out. Someone reached in and grabbed her. And they arrested the other one for attempted murder. They should have locked her up."

Karen's attempt to validate Clara's story also toned down the horror of the preceding story, in which the audience, not given the details to the contrary, assumed the woman had been killed. The listeners felt relief. They were pleased that the would-be murderer had been caught and that a Good Samaritan had intervened. No one questioned the authenticity of the story or its newspaper validation, even though in Clara's version, only three people were assumed to have been on the platform, and in Karen's version the incident supposedly happened during rush hour. Up to this point in the conversation, the women's stories included characters endemic to the urban scene. The cabbie, the loiterer, the ill-tempered subway rider, the Good Samaritan and the apathetic bystander are conventional characters in tales of New York City life. They are rarely given distinguishing features or personalities, yet they are the dramatis personae of these stories: since they are so well known, they are presented without any full explanations.

During the telling of Clara's story, Ann nodded affirmatively several times and then commented about the unexpected danger described in it. She said that after watching a television program in which a young chid was thrown off a rooftop, some neighborhood children had followed suit the next day by throwing a youngster over an apartment-building rooftop to his death. After all, she sighed knowingly, "Children *do* live on the roof in the summertime."

The above comment, as innocuous as it might seem, underlies another, unstated but significant, point about one of the functions of telling these urban tales: they impart street smarts. The audience accepts these stories without question because they reinforce something that they already know: being streetwise or street smart is essential when living in New York City. There is an urban folk wisdom, a common folk knowledge, about city living that New Yorkers possess. Surely, children do play pranks on one another, and those pranks often result in death. Rooftops *are* dangerous places indeed.

The women at the tea, typical of the tellers of crime-victim stories everywhere, used three narrative stances for reporting: (1) first-hand, or victim, accounts; (2) second-hand, or witness or bystander, accounts; and (3) third-hand accounts, in which the source of information is often a newspaper or television, or unknown—the speaker may use media accounts to validate or report a crime. The women changed narrative stances frequently and at random. This switching back and forth is a validating technique used to heighten the trustworthiness of a story as well as a feature of the oral style of reporting.

Shortly after Clara finished her story, Elizabeth, a member of the group, left for home. This interruption, however, did not change the conversations's direction: the women devoted the majority of the remaining time at the tea to exchanging crime-victim stories. The sharing and swapping between tellers increased. The atmosphere was competitive but not hostile. One incentive for relating stories was to tell one that was more horrible, more incredible, and more unpredictable than the last. Pam Day continued:

> This happened last November when our lease ran through. We were showing the apartment. One Sunday afternoon, I was alone . . . and there was a knock on the door, and somebody came to see the apartment. She was to

come at five o'clock. She showed up at five-thirty. I was a little teed off. But I opened the door, and she said, "Gee, I'm sorry to be late, but I've just been mugged!" [tone of disgust] She came by way of the IND subway to the Eighty-sixth Street stop, when a man followed her off and demanded her money. And she said, "Look, I'm giving you my money, but let me keep my wallet. You can't want my credit cards. You can't want my driver's license." So she was taking her money out of her wallet when he grabbed her wallet and pushed her down a flight of stairs! (**M-10**)

Both Clara's and Pam's stories highlight one of the important functions of transmitting crime-victim stories: they tell women how to protect themselves in case of danger. The story presented above tells how the victim used self-protection, most likely recalled from the other victim situations that she had heard about, or perhaps previously experienced. It also implies that the victim was unaware not only of the danger she was in, but of the inconvenience she was to face from the loss of her personal papers. Her behavior addressed both. In the other story, Clara said her technique to avoid danger would be to leave the subway: "I'd be out on the street in thirty seconds," she said sarcastically. Pams "victim" suggested not to fight with the mugger, but to submit and hand over the cash: "I'm giving you my money, but let me keep my wallet."

Once Pam finished, the conversation switched from crime-victim narratives to stories about crime-prevention techniques. What should a woman do in such a situation? How can people protect themselves? The women talked about the "weapons" to carry. Ann Holland advised carrying an umbrella: "One of the best things is the Totes umbrella, because it can collapse. They have a nice handle. When I carry an umbrella, I don't carry it by the handle strap. I carry it so that I can use it if I have to. . . . There are a lot of limping male sopranos in the city!" Pam admitted that to avoid being victimized, she usually "puts on the old poker face." But she acknowledged that this technique is not always successful:

About a year ago, let's see, I was taking a course at Marymount. I got home between ten and ten-thirty. I take a Number Ten bus at Eighty-fifth Street and Columbus Avenue. So one night I was going home, and I was walking on Central Park West to my apartment on Eighty-sixth Street. And this guy was coming up the other way. And he sorta looked at me and gave me the old, "How about it, dear?" And I put on my old stone face and walked, dat dat dat. . . . Got to my outer door . . . [and I go] to put the key into the front door, and *this hand* comes and grabs mine. He had turned around and followed me home, and I didn't look behind me. So I missed his little trick. So first, I just stood there in shock. And he said, "A little shy, are you?" And I said, "Oh my God! That's the way to the doorbells." And I said to him, "If you touch me, I'm gonna start ringing these doorbells!" So . . . he wanted a little action [nervous laughter]. So he went away. I mean, I didn't call the police even though I shoulda. I didn't even tell my roommate because I didn't want her to be afraid to go out on the streets. **(M-53)**

Pam's narrative about thwarting victimization by putting on the "old poker face" or learning that it is important to look over one's shoulder, and Ann's urban weapons approach reveal three crime-prevention techniques practiced by women on the city street. These stories also reiterate how one must be on guard living in the city world. By sharing these crime-prevention techniques, the women reinforced a bond among themselves. Pam's neglect to tell her roommate of the experience so as to preserve her roommate's sense of security in the neighborhood suggests that the stories' role in imparting street smarts is of major importance. As Susan Kalčik discusses in her work on women's rap groups, women often use "kernel stories" in conversation. These stories "emerge from the context in which they appear to support another woman's story, to help achieve a tone of harmony in the group, or to fit the topic under discussion or develop that topic with related ideas."[5] Both Ann's and Pam's explanations of their urban experience served this function, and they moved the conversation along.

Soon after the discussion of crime-prevention techniques calmed down, Irene Whitefield switched the topic to urban loiterers and told a story about a shopping-bag lady whom she had tried to direct to a church shelter. Then, Pam Day recalled an incident in which a shopping-bag man had trailed her through the New York Public Library while she was searching for a book. While both incidents could be seen as asides from crime-victim stories, they also deal with the social deviance of homeless people.[6] While their stories were not crime-victim events, the tellers used them as bridges between narratives. Shortly after Pam's comments about the homeless man, Karen Green jumped in with a story about another urban deviant—a loiterer who is suspected to be dangerous:

I'm on the seventh floor of a seven-story building, and there are steps to go to the roof, and there's nothing on the roof except tarpaper. For some obscure reason, people manage to get into the building. There's no intercom system, and there's just a buzzer. One night, the door buzzed, and we buzzed back because we had expected company. We go to the door and looked through the peephole. We see this body come up the steps, come off the elevator, and start looking around. So Rob [Karen's husband] stuck his head out of the door and said, "Get the hell out of here!" And the guy said, "If you come after me, I'm gonna knife you to death!" Rob quickly beat a fast retreat and shut the door. So we went and called the cops. In the meantime, the guy comes up the steps to the roof, and we hear shuffling around on the roof [group laughter]. So we go to the door again, and we're looking around the door—shuffle—shuffle [laughter]—and the guy comes down again to the seventh floor, and a light goes on when you push the elevator button. He pushed the button at the *exact* second that the cops hit the button. So you couldn't tell if someone downstairs was coming up. But you never saw anybody get such a *surprise in their entire life* when he's standing there to open the elevator door and there's these cops: *"All right, get outta here!"* [group laughter]

The audience cheered when Karen told them that the offender had been caught by the police. "He should have been locked up," she said emphatically.

Sensing sympathy from the women, Karen next recounted a burglary. "But I got robbed in my apartment a couple of years ago," she said. She provided the group with a laundry list of items that the burglars stole: "All my jewelry, my nursing school ring . . . the things they left behind I couldn't get over. . . . We had a digital radio and a table radio and a $125 35mm camera they never took and a tape recorder. . . . We had a Sony television and a quad stereo. . . . But all my husband's electric tools and my jewelry, two wedding rings, and my nursing school ring—STOLEN! I also had a fake diamond ring, BUT my garnet ring and my diamond earrings were left. Figure that one out!" At this point, Karen was overcome by emotion and nearly in tears.

Karen had presented her story as if it were a puzzle, asking the audience to help rationalize the offenders' actions. Karen thought that "maybe they were spooked" or disturbed during the robbery, and consequently left behind the items she listed. Clara suggested that perhaps "the heist" was a part of the burglars' "shopping around" for particular items. Still distraught from remembering the incident, Karen felt that insult had been added to injury when the burglars left her home with her valuables wrapped up in her own bedsheet!

As a coda to Karen's narrative, Clara retorted, "What good is money in New York?" Pam added, "I've seen people take Oriental rugs as they are going out over the rooftops!" "Where else but New York," they wondered, could such things happen? As the laughter subsided, Irene entered the competition. This time her cue was taken not from the previous narrator, but only from the content of the crime feat. Her opening statement acknowledges competition, suggested no doubt by the reference to the Oriental rug, the implication being that it was a large item for the sneaky thief:

> But I can top that one! In my apartment building where I lived before, two people who lived in my apartment before me—one was a pianist, a professional musician—[proceeds with slow and deliberate tone] and THEY STOLE THE GRAND!

Beginning with a robbery involving personal possessions with the victim in their midst, on to Oriental rugs, and then to the theft of a grand piano, Clara finished the robbery sequence in which not only large items were taken, but all the victim's possessions. These unbelievable but true stories delighted the audience immensely. Clara began:

> There was a guy I used to know at my old bank. His wife was going to the doctor. She was not well, and her four-year-old was away at nursery school. . . . He got a hysterical phone call from his wife that day. It was two o'clock. It turns out that on that morning a van rolled up, and two guys dressed in work clothes moved out all their furniture. *Everything!* The carpets, the lamps, clothing from the closet, contents of the medicine cabinet, books, magazines, TVs, radios, THE WORKS! When they came back to their apartment, there was NOTHING except the four empty walls! They did not take anything from the kid's room. That was completely intact. But every single thing was gone! Wall-to-wall rugs just ripped up and rolled away. EVERYTHING!

When Clara finished her story, several listeners tried to deduce the robber's motives. Laughing, one woman said, "Maybe they were setting up housekeeping!" Clara mentioned that the owners were convinced that "someone had been there and cased the place." No one in the group, however, had heard of the common technique of robbers' coming to a home disguised as workmen of some sort.[7]

By this time in the afternoon, several hours had passed, and the women soon went on to the affairs of the literary group. Their business discourse was distinctly separate from the previous swapping of crime-victim stories: the stories were regarded as part of the social discussion of the afternoon. After the business matters were concluded, several of the women left for home. They walked together to the subway, assuming safety in numbers.

The social setting in which these crime-victim stories were transmitted was not an unusual one for this group, or any other group of New Yorkers. The mundane setting underlines the horror of the stories. The cozy atmosphere of the social afternoon previously described contrasts sharply with the dangerous world of urban violence and victimization portrayed in the women's narratives. The depiction of urban life found in the crime-victim stories results in a common reporting technique, of which narrators are often unaware: the juxtaposition of narrative plots regardless of the severity of the crimes mentioned. For example, in the narrative setting just described, a mugging tale easily precedes a burglary story. What is being transmitted is not only a story about city life, but a shared perception of the effects of crime on city people and the need for safeguards against victimization. Because urbanites are aware of the possibilities of danger in the urban world, the theme of victimization easily connects the stories. Verbal cues from one story to another supply the invisible connective threads, while humor relieves the tension of the moment and enhances the personal interaction. The telling of crime-victim stories is a common outlet for diffusing fear, tension, and anger about an urban fact of life.

These stories not only highlight the need for street smarts (as Pam Day's stories underscore), they also present a world view shared by the women. They all expected New York City to be a dangerous place to live. Throughout the swapping of tales, several of the women made comments such as, "This is New York," or "Where else *but* New York?" Crime-victim stories reinforce common images associated with the urban setting, and these scenes are easily identified and visualized—a crowded subway platform, an empty rooftop above a busy street, a rider-crammed bus. The settings for these tales need no description or explanation: they are familiar places. They are urban *données*.

Crime-victim stories, in general, are an essential part of an ongoing urban socialization process, and are constant reminders to the audience and tellers that society's laws and urban customs need to be obeyed in order for cities, in this case New York City, to function smoothly. Yet these stories also have another purpose. They reiterate that not all members of society follow society's rules: some clearly and conspicuously defy the law. It is not only the physical violence in the stories that surprises the victims of crime and the audiences, it is also the offender's defiance and disregard of the law, his violation of the victim's personal space, or the stealing of a stranger's possessions that infuriates both victims and audience. Consequently, victims and potential victims, that is, listeners to the victim's stories, can learn about what it takes to live successfully in New York City. In other words, the crime-victim narrative is a testimonial to urban resilience. These stories celebrate survival. By sharing a story, the teller is proudly announcing, "I've survived! Here's my story!"

Most middle-class New Yorkers share personal experiences by using particular speech rules and speaking styles. For example, New Yorkers often abruptly enter into conversation, welcomed or not, with strangers and friends alike. Deborah Tannen, a sociolinguist, notes that "many New Yorkers . . . finding themselves within hearing range of a stranger's conversation . . . assume that it is appropriate to toss in a relevant comment."[8] Tannen suggests that in addition to "butting in," New Yorkers have a speech style and conversation pattern that includes other distinctive features. For example, they will abruptly introduce new topics of conversation. Often they insist on being heard, even demanding attention. Conversations usually revolve around personal topics in which the evaluative components are prominent. Tannen contends that in conversation, taking turns is popular, and talking is at bullet speed. Frequently during conversation, two or more New Yorkers will speak simultaneously, each eager to intrude with an opinion or personal example.

Many of Tannen's assumptions about the conversational style of New

Yorkers were validated during that afternoon while the women traded crime-victim stories. Interruptions of their conversation, however, occurred in two ways. The women would periodically wander into the dining room for refreshments and back into the living room where the conversations were taking place. Because of the relaxed atmosphere, they freely entered and left conversations, and when returning to the room, they quickly jumped back into them. The other interruptions had more to do with the conventions of New York City speech. As Tannen mentions, one of the rules for New York conversation allows several speakers to talk simultaneously. While the noise level might be high, the practice of two or more people speaking at the same time is more of an indication of enthusiasm for the topic at hand than a display of rudeness.[9] However, during the women's discussion, and as the crime-victim stories became the central focus of the conversation, the atmosphere in the room changed. Only the narrator spoke, and the audience listened. So, despite the New York City "all-talk" style, each narrator drew attention to herself and to her story. The style of conversation switched from many speakers to only one, thus emphasizing the narrator and her story.

For example, Ann's story about the policeman was a conversational icebreaker told for entertainment. To be amusing, the tellers of these stories, like Ann, often give them a sharp edge by narrating them in an abrasive, witty manner. This type of biting invective is a form of urban folk humor, especially popular in New York City. It is known to popular-culture audiences through such comics as Joan Rivers, Robert Klein, Rodney Dangerfield, and Woody Allen. These comedians grew up in urban areas and derive many of their routines from common aspects of city life: rudeness towards others, the constant violation of personal space, the variety of types of people found in the urban environment, the conflicts that result because of multicultural groups, the difficulties of dealing with city bureaucracy, and, of course, urban crime. In one of his nightclub acts, Rodney Dangerfield remarks about the dangers of living on Manhattan's Upper West Side: "I live in the only neighborhood that when I plan my budget, I allow for holdup money." His line is like Pam's story about the woman who was mugged in Pam's Upper West Side apartment building.

The popularity of this urban comedy results from an understanding between comedians and audiences that city life requires an urban invulnerability and a need to look out for and guard against unexpected danger. The stories told during the afternoon were often accepted with laughter, functioning in a way similar to the urban comic's material. Both expect that urbanites, in order to live in the city, will need several essential psychological tools: a sense of empathy towards crime victims but an ability to distance oneself from and even laugh at another's misfortunes; a sense of self-acceptance, especially if one has been victimized; and, finally, realization and acceptance that individuals alone cannot stop the city's and nation's crime epidemic.

Discussing stories within a particular sociocultural context, such as the afternoon gathering analyzed here, is one method that we can use to make intelligent assumptions and suggestions about how folklore and urban folk traditions appear within the context of everyday life. Crime-victim stories are more structured, more polished, and more traditional than most narrators and audiences realize. In both organization and style, they tend to utilize traditional narrative conventions. When stories related by different tellers are compared, similarities emerge in form as well as content. In addition, crime-victim narratives can be disguised as another form of folk story, the urban legend. In suggesting ways that urbanites can protect themselves from crime, these stories serve a particular function by imparting knowledge about appropriate urbanite street behavior. They also reveal how New York City is presented by those who fear it, by those who love it, and by those who have experienced its danger.

CHAPTER TWO

The Traditional Components of the Crime-Victim Narrative

Victimization and crime prevention are among the most popular and traditional topics of conversation for New Yorkers. The crime-victim stories are within the realm of believable daily experience. Meeting up with a street criminal, hearing about a neighborhood murder, or witnessing a violent attack is seen as an unpleasant contingency of living in a large metropolitan center. The crimes these stories deal with are primarily street muggings, rape, and murder, in that order of frequency. Only two of the many possible outcomes are emphasized: survival and death. Unprovoked or senseless violence, untimely death, escape from danger, suspicion of others, and bystander apathy are all plot elements of crime-victim stories. The central and recurring themes are the ability to think quickly on one's feet, take control of a dangerous situation, discover one's vulnerability—even mortality, and accept victimization as part of urban life.

The possibility of meeting with a sudden, violent death because of a chance encounter with an unknown, armed stranger is the underlying theme of these narratives. Relating them invokes a common outcry of moral outrage against such gratuitous violence. These stories express indignation about what tellers perceive as a decline in the social order; they are a cry against antisocial violence and behavior. But perhaps more important, they emphasize the value our culture places on life and self-protection, an emphasis that makes them culturally significant. Most tellers present offenders who inflict harm and then escape unpunished. In other folk narratives, punishment is meted out against the antagonist for violating a law or breaking some taboo, thus maintaining the social order.[1]

In contemporary crime-victim narratives, it is this very lack of punishment, this failure of the legal system, that provokes the victim/teller's outrage. As a result, the primary focus of these stories is surviving the criminal assault; the theme of punishment is emphasized much less.[2]

THE GENERAL FEATURES OF THE CRIME-VICTIM STORY

The crime-victim story may take several forms, depending on the narrative stance of the teller. A story told by the victim tends to be lengthy and elaborately detailed; folklorists often call this form a memorate, a remarkable-experience story that may evolve into an urban legend. When told by a second-hand reporter, such as a victim's relative or friend, the tale tends to be shorter and the descriptive scenes condensed. Even so, these stories are neither less dramatic nor very different from first-hand accounts. When stories are told by second-hand reporters who know only snatches of the details, and do not know the victim personally, the plot is emphasized.

While these third-person stories may seem like skeletons of narratives, or what William Labov would describe as "minimal narratives," tellers clearly identify them as stories, and not mere incidents.[3] "I have a story to tell you," a teller often says, and follows the remark by relating a string of connected events, perhaps several incidents that occurred during the course of a day. "Stories" or "tales" included here are structured, have a plot, and are viewed as a native category by the informants. Personal-experience stories about victimization are recapitulations of criminallike experiences that may or may not contain traditional folklore content. However, they are similar in narrative content, structure, and style to one another.[4] Personal-experience narratives of crime victims or people associated with them may sometimes be told as anecdotes, but only rarely are they transformed into jokes.[5]

Similar to other categories of culture-bound narratives, such as the ethnic or the occupational personal-experience narrative, the crime-victim story falls into subcategories and has specific narrative characters.[6] The first subcategory contains narratives about urban crime experiences that victims believed were caused by a stroke of bad luck, i.e., by being "in the wrong place at the wrong time." A second subcategory includes stories about bystander apathy, where witnesses are too fearful to intervene in ongoing crimes. Each story has some "telltale sign" that indicates its placement in that particular subcategory.[7] These signs can be expressed in the victim's words, by how the victim acts in relationship to the other story characters, or by the teller's evaluative comments about the characters, expressed in narrative asides as the story is being told. For example, the teller might say that the offender acted unwisely or was extremely vicious.

In addition to specific narrative subcategories, crime-victim stories have stock characters, one of the earmarks of traditional narrative.[8] Though statistical studies show that most murders take place between persons who know one another, crime-victim narratives project fear of an anonymous criminal, a stranger lurking in a dark alleyway ready to pounce on an innocent victim.[9] Like the ogre and bogeyman of older folktales, this stereotypical urban character evokes an ill-defined fear of physical assault and danger.[10] In the crime-victim stories, stock characters, both as offenders and as victims, are commonly portrayed as tricksters. The trickster has long been a familiar type in folklore,[11] and it is not surprising that this character would appear in contemporary narrative. Tricksters typically escape from threatening situations, and like con men, they are common in the urban scene and its literature.[12]

In crime-victim stories, the victim protagonists are generally people who meet up with an unfortunate situation. They often insist that they abused or misunderstood a common rule or folkway of urban life, such as allowing a "friendly" stranger to enter a locked building behind them or using an elevator without being wary of fellow passengers.

> I had a friend, and this is when I was living in Manhattan. She went to visit a friend who was living on the sixth floor. They were going up the elevator, and it stopped at three. A guy comes in, and the elevator started going up again. She started to walk out, and this guy stepped out and stabbed her in the back. She didn't feel the stab. It was like a sharp pierce. Just missed her spinal cord. . . . **(M-68)**

Victim protagonists often appear as trusting, polite, and law-abiding citizens who follow the accepted rules of public behavior. Many victims in these stories are sophisticated urbanites who have a repertory of crime-prevention skills and techniques, but whose cultural knowledge of how to behave in an urban environment fails when put to the test. They do not see themselves as urban bunglers, and are surprised that they were victimized. In fact, a common phrase is, "I thought this would never happen to me." Most victims for this study repeated only a handful of incidents about themselves, which they saw as isolated in their own lives but as part of the collective experience of urbanites. When the victim protagonists are not the narrators, tellers often portray the victims as naive, and they are consequently unsympathetic towards them. These characters are viewed as "city greenhorns" who lack street smarts. On occasion, especially if tricked by an offender, victims may describe themselves in such terms as well.[13]

The offender antagonists are usually depicted as secondary characters in these stories, although it is their presence that provides the narrative with its raison d'être. The offender is often presented either as a stupid, unthinking person, or as a crafty manipulator who delights in preying on innocent victims. Offenders take the victim by surprise, appearing almost out of nowhere. These antagonists are the anonymous and fearsome stock characters of the stories.

Crime-victim stories emphasize more than the chance encounter between victim and offender; they show that victimizations take place in common settings. Most of the story events occur in public places, but in areas where entrapment is easy.[14] As one informant said, "It's the kind of thing when you are in an elevator and you are trapped, and someone comes in and you really can't get out."[15] The recurring settings include the elevator, the subway, the apartment lobby or vestibule, the public street, and the public park. Ironically, the criminal incidents often occur in the midst of ongoing urban activity, such as a mugging happening in front of the Public Library or on a busy street filled with passersby. For example, a narrator may mention that he or she was being robbed while others were walking past, unaware of the moment of jeopardy: "There were people who were walking by, and they saw what was going on, and there was a policeman on the corner, but he just kept walking," said one informant.[16] Victims sometimes express their anger about having to live in a city where physical assault or verbal abuse is so frequently a part of the lifestyle, it is accepted as commonplace. For example, Susan Roberts recalls an incident in which she was molested by a fellow subway rider at a busy mid-Manhattan subway station:

> People on the escalator saw the entire thing happen. It was a quarter to nine in the morning, and I was going to school. And they just stood and watched. Stood there. And I was screaming hysterically. Stood there. . . . This one woman sort of came up and got a cop. And their reaction was, we [the Samaritan and the cop] know you are upset because you are embarrassed by the situation. I was trying to tell them I wasn't embarrassed but that this pervert did this crazy thing to me and I was screaming for help! **(R-11)**

Significantly, the informant's comment includes several themes of the crime-victim narrative genre: the incident occurred in a public setting; she was accosted within an enclosed environment, the escalator; several people witnessed the event, and only one offered help; and, finally, the situation had an unsettling and powerful effect on her. When she told the story, her anger was obvious; her voice was shrill, her face taut.

The public or semipublic settings of the stories are familiar and comfortable to the victims because they use them everyday. They therefore are perceived not as dangerous, but rather as places to be trusted. In fact, a common theme is the victim's surprise that he or she could be harmed or violated in such familiar surroundings.[17] For example, Norma Schultz overheard a conversation between a mugger and his victim in the elevator of her apartment building, where she had been a tenant for over forty years:

> We had a mugging in this house with a knife. It was in the elevator. I thought I saw him. I was here with Clara. I had taken her for a haircut, and we were waiting for the elevator. While the elevator was going up, I thought I heard someone say in the elevator . . . as it went by . . . "I want it now!" But that didn't mean anything to me. Then we waited for the elevator to come down, and someone. . . . But when the elevator came back, as I was opening the door, I heard somebody coming down the steps. I turned around to look, and there was this man. A young boy. No shirt on. And I thought I saw him put a big kitchen knife in the back of his pants. But I thought I must be seeing things, and he looked at us and he ran off. But I wasn't sure who he was, and I didn't say anything to her, and I took care of my business, and that was all.
>
> When I came home that night, I thought I must have imagined all this. The next night I ran into Frances Fried, my neighbor. She said, "Did you hear what happened?" She said there was a young man, Hispanic man, no shirt on, who was standing downstairs outside of the building. It was about two o'clock in the afternoon. There were people around. There were women with baby carriages and playing with the babies. They all got into the elevator together. One got off on the second floor. One got off on the fourth floor. And one got off on the sixth floor—[he] held a knife to her throat and took her purse. And he said, "Don't call anybody for at least ten minutes, or I'll come back and kill you." She didn't say anything. Later, she went to Frances Fried. The woman was Russian, and I don't think she speaks English well. And they called the police. But who are you gonna catch?
> **(M-24)**

The incident described above occurred at two o'clock on a sunny afternoon. The young man appeared outside of the apartment building, where many mothers congregate and talk while pushing their babies to sleep in their carriages. He had garnered their trust by chatting with the women and admiring their children. Within a few minutes, he gained entrance into the locked building. That the incident took place in such familiar territory was a surprise to Norma, for it violated her belief that places used daily are safe places. She refused to see herself as an urban bungler, rationalizing that she had misjudged the situation. She was surprised to have been witness to violence, and at first even refused to acknowledge that the offender had a weapon. These themes present in Norma's story are common to other, similar crime-victim stories.

The victims in these stories often die a senseless and meaningless death or are needlessly harmed, in contrast to the hero character in the American folk tradition, who may die a tragic death because he has broken some cultural taboo that supersedes an act of bravery. For example, in the Anglo-American occupational ballad tradition, death usually results from an accident, and the rationale for death is the violation of the heroic code.[18] These occupational songs teach about the results of carelessness, recklessness, or overwork.[19] Such rationalizations are missing in these crime stories, where death is violent and shocking. The stories remind the audience that violent death occurs not only in the world of glamorous television detectives or underworld figures, but also in the world of the ordinary citizen. In the first example given below, one driver shoots and kills another on a Brooklyn street corner because he thought he was being cut off in traffic. In the second story, the motive is unclear. These stories are not sentimentalized, but are presented in sad and tragic terms and in gruesome detail. Victims have little chance of defending themselves, and motives for the crimes are often unknown. So, it is up to the listeners and narrators to make sense out of the baffling events. Because the stories involve the untimely death of a victim, the tellers may begin to reevaluate their own lives, much like a patient recovering from a serious illness. After all, knowing about such violent events may provide the first opportunity for individuals to discover their own vulnerability and mortality. The listeners may show sympathy for the victim's plight and may also express shock at the story's events. The themes of senseless violence, untimely death, death without reason, and the reversal of an everyday routine because of crime, appear in the following two stories. The first is about a man in his early twenties:

> This happened several months ago. . . . The young man picked up his friend, and they were going somewhere. This happened on Flatbush, on the corner of Cortelyou and Flatbush. They were about to make a turn, and this other car came by. And they [the first driver and his passenger] were standing in line, but evidently the other car thought he [the first driver] cut him [the second driver] off. So, he [the second driver] pulled up on the side of him and shouted all sorts of obscenities. They didn't even answer him. The next thing he [the first driver] knew, he [the second driver] pulled out a gun and shot him [the first driver] and drove away. And he left the friend with a fellow who was dead, and he [the passenger] didn't even know it. They started to drive away. The car was moving forward, and they crashed into a tree. And then he realized he was dead. He died from a gunshot. That's it. (MR-18)

The second narrative was collected from Roberta Wolf and Norma Schultz in Brooklyn. Both women contributed to its telling. The victim was a neighbor, a young religious woman.

> You heard about the Chassidic girl that got killed in this building? The girl was killed in the city. It was the worker's son—the elevator operator or

something. . . . The Chassidic pregnant girl—who got crushed to death, or they found her in a garbage can or something. . . . It happened in the Garment Center. She had gone to New York to buy a coat for her mother. . . . And she didn't return. And they went to New York. But she had not returned. It was during the week. And they couldn't find her. And they went looking around. Then finally somebody noticed there was a carton outside the building that was dripping blood. They opened it up, and they found a part of her. . . . It seems that she had gotten into the elevator. And the elevator had been slow, and she said to him, "Why don't you hurry up?" It was somebody she knew. And it seems that he was eating his lunch, . . . he was very annoyed and irritated by the bells ringing. He took her down to the basement, he raped her and sodomized her and stuffed her into the furnace. . . . And then he tired to dismember her. But they caught him, and they had the trial, and half of the neighborhood was there. She had a tremendous funeral. (**MR-5**)

The above two stories emphasize the unpredictable actions of the antagonists and the senselessness of each death. The situations in which both victims found themselves are very common. One was battling city traffic, and the other was dealing with the abuses of elevator etiquette. A common motif of the crime-victim stories involving murder is the reversal of an everyday situation: a benign moment turned into a scene of unexpected danger. Death without sufficient provocation is another common motif.

While unprovoked danger and murder are prevalent themes in these stories, another is the suspicion city dwellers have of those around them, sometimes without cause. Many of the stories deal with street smarts: awareness of the environment and any elements of danger, and the ability to act accordingly. In other words, victims insist on the importance of following one's intuition. In the followng example, the victim is described as a "city greenhorn," a person who should have been suspicious but wasn't, and paid the consequences:

She was walking down the street one evening. She saw three or four kids coming towards her and she said . . . she was thinking to herself . . . "Why not go across the street." You know, 'cause you never know. But she started thinking why should she do that because there are just four kids walking down the street. Well, they got her! One had a knife and took her money and all that. (**M-20**)

Since these crime-victim stories are so much a part of the city's oral tradition, and because victimization is perceived as common by the tellers, they stress that being on one's guard is an important part of one's urban behavior. Clara Gold of Brooklyn told the following story:

I'm coming home from the Metropolitan Opera two weeks ago, and I'm walking around with three hundred bucks in cash. Five o'clock, six o'clock at night. It's pitch black. I'm walking around Grand Army Plaza [Brooklyn]. It's freezing cold. Nobody in the street. So instead of walking around the Plaza itself, I walk around Plaza Street, where at least they have houses and doormen. And I hear footsteps behind me. It's still pretty deserted. So, I'm looking around, and there's this black kid about seventeen or eighteen [years old]. Now, if you're a New Yorker, any person between the ages of fourteen and twenty-two is immediately suspect anyway, whether they are black, white, green, pink, or orange, if they're male especially. And as this kid comes up level with me, I turn around and look at him again, and he looks at me and nods and smiles and says, "Don't worry, lady, I'm a cop!" He keeps on going. I started to laugh. I really cracked up. I said, "Okay, two points! You got me!" I felt kind of chagrined, but I laughed because obviously he could tell the state of my mind. He must be pretty used to it all at this stage of the game, too. **(M-70)**

The narrator's amusement afforded her a sense of relief, and she was able to recognize her own "paranoia." Her laughter rippled through her rendition of the story. She was relieved, yet concerned and frightened. But sometimes, misjudging others, as Clara did, can have unpredictable results:

We were sitting on the subway [station], and this man came walking in not paying his fare. And the man in the booth called him, and he said, "I have no money. I just came from the hospital." What he was doing here when he came from Coney Island Hospital, I don't know. . . . And we got up on the train [platform], and we walked away from him as far as possible. He looked peculiar. He had black eyes, and he was black and blue. He didn't look right. And we thought he was drunk or something. And we got on the train. And then he sat down right opposite us. So, we paid no attention to him. Then, he asked us a question about where the train was going, because they were very irregular because they are fixing the tracks. So, being polite . . . we told him the train was going the way the N train was going. He said, "That's good. I have to go to Fourteenth Street. I just got out of Coney Island Hospital. You wouldn't believe it, but my wife and I were on the B line train. We got off at Seventy-first Street on the B line; Seventy-first and New Utrecht Avenue. And four young men about twenty-five years old," he said. "I'm thirty-one," he said. "They were almost my age." He said they were at least twenty-five. "Nicely dressed young men got up, asked me for money," and he said, "What do you want my money for?" And they started to beat him up and his wife. They blackened her eyes. They cut him with a knife across his forehead. He picked up his hair to show us the cut [gestures]. And he said that he was in the hospital for a week and a half. They took $140 from his wife and $80 from him. But these were white, nice Italian boys. He said they were most likely Italian boys. They looked like nice Italians. It was in an Italian neighborhood. And they beat him unmercifully and cut him and all. He said that they only blackened his wife's eyes. They didn't hurt her more than that. But they hit her and slapped her around, too. And he said he was very angry. He said he had a little five-year-old-boy, and he asked, "Daddy, why did they do that to you?" And he said, "They were bad people." He tried to explain it to the child. But you know, so the child shouldn't be so fearful. It just happened. But here was this man, and we were so afraid, and he was a victim. **(M-81)**

In the above narrative, the teller, Esther Silverman, a woman in her mid-sixties, makes it clear that she and her companion avoided the man: "He didn't look right." At first, the man acted strangely; he did not pay his fare, and his appearance was peculiar. When they discovered that he would not harm them, but had been harmed himself, they sympathized. While telling her story, Esther discussed her wariness towards the victim. Then after the revelation, she expressed compassion towards him and his family. It was because she and her friend identified with the victim that they could make this turnaround; however, tellers are not always that empathetic.[20]

NARRATIVE CATEGORIES

The Fated Victimization

The prognostication of good and bad luck and the belief in omens and signs have long been a part of the American folk tradition, and are generally regarded as a response or desire to control the future. When good things happen, Americans often attribute their success to luck. When bad things happen, such as the loss of the family fortune, the assumption is that fate has stepped in to precipitate a reversal of luck.[21] Since street muggings are seldom premeditated, victims often surmise that they were just "in the wrong place at the wrong time." By relying on fate and ill fortune, they can then absolve themselves of blame. In the following example, the teller, a second-hand reporter, attributes the victim's unfortunate experiences to being "in the wrong place at the wrong time":

There's another one that was in the paper at Columbia. This sophomore girl . . . took the Number Three train instead of the Number One. Instead of getting off at Ninety-sixth [Street], changing for the local [subway] to get off at Columbia [University] she stayed on. She got off on 116th Street. The numbers are the same, I think: 103, 110, 116, except they're on Lexington Avenue. VERY BAD. It's on the other side of Morningside Park. She got out and realized her mistake. It was about five o'clock in the afternoon. She decided to walk through the park. On the way, she met this gang of boys, about five or six of them, aged ten to maybe eighteen. They all successively raped her. She got raped like a few times by the gang. Then she started to run away after they were done and got stopped another time by this huge guy. He raped her. And then she ran the rest of the way home. She got raped like four times in the same afternoon. It was written up in the *Spectator*

[Columbia University student newspaper]. She was interviewed about a week later. She said it didn't bother her. She just realized what the situation was, and she was in the wrong. She wasn't traumatized by it at all. She said, "I was in the wrong place at the wrong time. I made a mistake, and this weird thing happened to me." (R-3)

This narrative about such a horribly violent experience is significant for several reasons. The story is a recapitulation of an event that the teller first heard about in print and then refashioned into an oral account. It indicates that the acceptance of such a vicious crime can be the result of fate or destiny: "She said, 'I was in the wrong place at the wrong time.' " The narrator would have us believe, then, that her offenders are without blame. And the narrator—not the victim—makes the summation, "She just realized what the situation was, and she was in the wrong." This in no way implies that rape is not a traumatic or brutal experience. However, it is the narrator, a young woman of twenty-three, who makes the assumption that the rape victim was not traumatized by what happened to her. The teller implies not only that the subway ride was a dangerous one, but also that the error of taking the wrong train was in a sense responsible for the subsequent events. Characters, then, can be portrayed unsympathetically, and informants may blame them for not following their intuition, or for making some error in judgment, such as getting lost, not knowing safe areas from unsafe ones, or not following their intuition. These urban greenhorns, as they appear in these stories, commit such blunders. But many times, second-hand reporters do identify with the victims, as the example below shows:

This happened to Jean, one of my neighbors. It was funny, because I was coming in the lobby. I probably came home about six-thirty that night, and I walked into the lobby of my building, and there is the neighbor from downstairs and an apartment over. She's sitting on one of the chairs in the lobby. And two other neighbors are talking to her. And it looked like a fairly unusual situation. And as I walked in I said, "Something happen?" She had just been mugged. She was at the corner of Montgomery and Prospect Park West, and two kids, two black kids, ran up to her. This was Halloween, and there had just been a spate of egg-throwing incidents. Kids from across the street had been throwing eggs at people who had been coming home from work. And she was coming home from work. Two kids came up to her, grabbed her purse, and vanished into the park. She was sitting downstairs because she didn't have a key to her apartment. She couldn't get in. Her brother and sister-in-law live in the neighborhood, and she had tried to phone them so they could come over to let her in with their key. She was waiting for them to let her in. She hadn't been hurt or anything. It was just very frightening. And the amazing thing was that I walked past, it must have been ten minutes after she had gotten mugged, and absolutely nothing. People were walking around as if nothing had happened. I didn't see anything. I didn't hear anything. And I literally missed it by five or ten minutes. **(M-88)**

Clara Gold's story about her neighbor highlights the possibility that Clara herself could have been the victim. During our interview, she said anxiously, "And the amazing thing was that I walked past, it must have been ten minutes after she had gotten mugged, and [I saw] absolutely nothing." In this example, Clara provides several of the themes found in many of these narratives: the unpredictability of being a victim, fear and apprehension toward others, and personal inconvenience because of victimzation.

Bystander Apathy

A common complaint of many New Yorkers is bystander apathy, and its prominence as a narrative category and motif in these stories is not surprising. The unwillingness to become involved in a crime-victim situation is one of the trademarks of urban city life. Studies on bystander apathy, one, in particular, by Bibb Latané and John Darley, indicate that emergency situations are clearly related to the witnesses' concept of responsibility. When several people witness an event as a group, each person assumes that another group member will intervene, and consequently no one person acts or assumes responsibility. In other words, the more bystanders that witness an emergency, the less help the victim receives:[22]

> I saw a bunch of guys who were about twenty or twenty-five. One of them was chasing another with a knife. I saw the blade flash, you know, the white flash of the metal. And I saw them chasing him. And there was a crowd just standing on the stoops [of a building], and they didn't run after them. They were just—THEY WERE JUST WATCHING THE WHOLE THING! JUST WATCHING THE WHOLE THING! I didn't see a cop around at all. And they were just WATCHING THE WHOLE THING! **(M-47)**

The narrator of this story, Robert Ross, was one of several narrators who were outraged at the indifference citizens showed towards one another; yet he himself did not jump in to aid the victim. The role-reversal theme that appears in this story and the one below is prominent in these bystander apathy stories. Some informants were infuriated by the bystanders' lack of responsibility towards the victims, but they themselves exhibited this same feature.[23] In the example below, the narrator, Marvin Woltz, carries the motif of bystander indifference further: "There was a policeman on the corner, but he just kept walking." While Ross expects assistance from the police, Woltz complains that their presence does not,

in this case, make a difference. The example below was recalled sixteen
years after it happened:

> And I bought some things in Klein's [department store], and I headed over
> to May's, and I was looking in the window. And I turned around, and these
> two big black guys were standing there with hunting knives in my stomach.
> Yeah, they were hunting knives. *No* exaggeration over the years. And they
> asked for my money. There were people who were walking by, and they saw
> what was going on, and there was a policeman on the corner, but he just
> kept walking. Also there was a guy sitting reading a book. . . . And he just
> looked over and continued reading his book. . . . And then, let's see, they
> took my money—my twenty-two dollars. They took me down to the subway
> and left me there. . . . (M-27)

Bystander indifference and the expectation of victimization are two common themes of these stories.

CHARACTER TYPES

The Trickster Offender

A character type common to the crime-victim stories is the offender
who poses as a trickster. This offender is manipulative, scheming, and
cunning, and preys on the weaknesses and vulnerabilities of his victims.
He dons several disguises, posing most often as the friendly neighbor. He
is unpredictable, demanding, even childlike, and he is quick to anger. The
offender is usually dangerous because he is able to physically overpower
his victim, and is often armed. The following narrative illustrates several
features of the trickster character. First, he appears as the friendly neighbor, revealing a childlike insistence on doing a good deed. The narrator of
the story focuses on its trickster twist. The transformation of the friendly
neighbor into the manipulative, violent man who nearly murders his
victim infuses drama into the story, and turns an everyday event into a
horrifying one.

> There was one incident I heard. A woman comes home from Florida on
> her vacation. And as the taxi man left the bags on the curb . . . there were
> two bags . . . a young fellow came over to her and said, "Can I help you
> with the bags?" He says, "I live in the building." She says, "No." She says,
> "I can manage." He says, "Oh, those are too heavy for you. I'll help you
> up." So she figured, "well, he was nice enough to offer to help her up, so she
> let him do it. So he helped her up, and she opens the door, and he brings the
> bags in for her, and then he said, "Good-bye." And she said, "Thank you
> very much. Can I offer you some money?" He says, "No, not at all." He

says, "It's only a good neighbor policy," and went out. And she thought to herself, "Gee, what a nice young man that is."

The next day the bell rings. So she opens the door, but she has it on the chain lock. And he says, "Do you remember me? I'm the young fellow that helped you with the bags." So she said, "Yes, what is it?" He says, "Well, when I came in with the bags I dropped a ring here, and I want to know if you found it." She says, "No, I didn't find anything." And he said, "Well, would you mind if I look, because it was loose, and I know that I dropped it here." So she didn't think anything of it. So she opened the door. He came in, and he took her jewelery, beat her to a pulp, and then ransacked her house and walked out and closed the door. That's another gimmick they have. **(M-1)**

The return of the man to find his ring, a gimmick he uses to gain entry, adds the twist to the story. The victim who "didn't think anything of it" was duped because of her own sense of trust in the man. The coda to the story—"That's another gimmick they have"—suggests that a well-known fact of urban life is being transmitted. The offender is wearing the mask of the "friendly neighbor" as well as the "Good Samaritan," and seemingly wishes only to aid the intended victim in some task. The common characteristics of the trickster—manipulative, preyful, deceitful—appear in several of these collected narratives:

There was one incident where a friend of mine came to the elevator, and a young fellow said to her, he says, "I think I have friends that live on the fifth floor." So he says, "Do you know this party?" So she says, "No, I don't. He says, "Well, what floor are you going to?" She says, "Well, actually I'm going to go to the third floor." He says, "Well, I'm going to look for this party." And she went into the elevator alone, and he went 'round up the steps. When he saw the elevator didn't stop on the third floor, he ran up to the fourth floor. The elevator stopped, and he caught her just as she got out of the elevator. He beat her up very badly, and she was in a wheelchair for quite a few months. It is really pitiful. **(M-12)**

The initial harmlessness of the offender provides the story with the added twist needed to remember it. The mugging happened in an enclosed area and in territory familiar to the victim. She courteously responded to a simple request made by the man, who asked a common question. The assumption by the narrator, Ruth Melberg, is that the trickster is totally amoral. Ruth provides no rationale for the attack but suggests that a display of physical violence by the offender is a possible motive. The theme of gratuitous violence, common to many of these stories, is highlighted.

Female trickster offenders use the same devious methods as their male counterparts.[24] The offender often appears friendly and attempts to share the same territory as the victim, and then suddenly tricks him or her and turns on her prey. In the following crime-victim narrative, the assailant is a black woman in her mid-twenties. She introduced herself to her victim, Esther Silverman, by pretending to look for another neighbor. Both the lobby vestibule and the elevator, two confined areas, provided the setting for the entrapment. The victim had positive sentiments toward the physical environment; she felt safe, since she had been a tenant of the building for more than thirty years. The trickster (and others like her) manipulated her victim by winning her trust. The victim, a retired schoolteacher in her mid-sixties, anxiously discussed the viciousness of the attack:

> It was in April, 1983. I was on a sabbatical, and I was taking courses at Kingsborough College. This was the day I didn't have classes. And I went shopping. I came back at three o'clock in the afternoon carrying two bags of groceries. And there was a woman in the lobby who was looking at names [on the building register], and she said, "Do you know that sick person, the sick man?" And I said,"Oh, you mean the man on the third floor?" And she said, "Yes." And I said, "He's on the third floor. I think he's in Apartment 3C." She said,"That's the one I need." We have a lot of black ladies, young ladies, taking care of sick and old people here in the building. So, she opened the elevator door for me, and I got in. And as soon as the door closed, she took out a pistol and hit me on the head with it. And I said to her, "What the hell are you hitting me for? Here's my pocketbook!" So she pushed the first floor [button] again, and she said, "Don't yell!" And I said, "I'm not yelling. What good would yelling do me in the elevator?" And she got out. She hit me several times. I have a picture that the police took, and I was all bruised from a pistol-whipping on the head. I gave her my pocketbook. And she ran out. Sent me down to the basement. When I came up I ran out, but I couldn't find her. I went looking for her. Then I came up here [to her apartment], and by that time I began to be in real bad pain. I got ice and I put it to my head, and I called the police. . . . (M-79)

Shortly after reporting the incident, she was asked to go down to the precinct house, where she met several of the offender's other victims, who had strikingly similar incidents to report.

The Clever Victim

The clever victim, another common character of these crime-victim stories, is the trickster's foil. Faced with a dangerous situation, the clever victim acts in a level-headed yet devious fashion, trying all the time to elude the offender. In some instances, the clever victim has been mugged previously and as a result has taken precautions. For example, victims might carry "mugger money," just in case they meet up with danger. One informant, Mary Simmons of Brooklyn, discussed her brother's experiences:

My brother carries mugger money. He puts his money—like he put a dollar bill in his pocket 'cause he lives on Church and Ocean Avenues [Brooklyn]. . . . He has been mugged several times. So what does he do? So, he carries like a dollar in his pocket and his wallet someplace else. He was stopped just recently. He told me the story. A bunch of kids circled him into the middle. They said, "Give me your money!" One of them had a knife or something. He said, "I only have a dollar. I was going for the paper." He had a wallet with money in it. But he put his hand into his pocket and said, "Here, look in my pocket." And he emptied both of his pockets. He said, "Here, all I have is the dollar. I'm going to get the paper." They took the dollar. And they left him alone. He carried that dollar purposely. He's been mugged several times. He's never been hurt. He's been lucky. And that was that. (**M-66**)

Studies show that muggers act spontaneously, and seldom think of the consequences of breaking the law.[25] In the above narrative, the victim is the schemer, prepared for danger. His sister makes it clear that in his several experiences with this urban ritual, he has been lucky and has not been seriously hurt. That he has been "lucky" reinforces the theme of the fateful encounter engendered in so many of these stories.

In the following narrative, the victim trickster takes on the muggers single-handedly. Two common themes appear: the mugger pretends to belong in the environment, and the victim responds by upholding the laws of urban civility. But like most narratives in this category, this one has a twist. The teller gives details of setting, place, and time that provide some orientation to how the mugging was thwarted. Unlike the previous victim, who carried mugger money as an urban survival tactic, this next victim underscores the surprise of being singled out as a victim. Here, Bobbi Taylor boasts about her ability to think quickly on her feet. She assumes a knowledge of the motive for the mugging—drugs. Like other victims, she is angry at being a target.

This was when I was living on the Lower East Side on Seventh Street between Avenues B and C. This was many years ago . . . probably around the late 1960s. . . . I was coming from Hunter College. I had just been having one of my marathon sessions with a professor . . . for my master's thesis. And I had a ton of books that I was carrying in my arms. Both arms. Those were the days when I didn't have a book bag. People didn't have book bags then. I had a little purse that was sort of stuck down between my books and my bust. I had a dollar. That's all I had was a dollar. And so I got off the subway, and I took the Avenue B bus, and I got off at Avenue B between Seventh and Eighth streets. And it was late. It was like eleven, eleven-thirty at night. So, I'm walking to my house. We didn't have a lock on the front door. So I just pushed the door with my shoulder, which is what I always did. And I didn't have hands because I was carrying books. And there were two guys behind me, and they looked like friends of upstairs neighbors. So I held the door for them. Both doors, the outside door and the inside door. I held the door for them because I'm a polite person. Then I start trudging up the stairs with my armful of books and the one dollar in my purse stuck between my books and my bosom. And the next thing I know is that these guys are real close behind me, and I feel a hand over my mouth. And he starts to pull me. At first, I was angry. I opened the door for this mother-fucker! I got real angry. He does this after I open the door for him! I thought, I only have a dollar. Let me give him the dollar. Then, no, I thought. He'll kill me. That's not enough for a fix. And so I could feel he was shorter than me 'cause he was reaching up. He had a hand up against my mouth. So I just let myself fall back. We went bouncing down a flight of stairs with him underneath me. He was a little shrimpy fellow. And his partner took off as soon as he saw us coming. And he looked up at me. And then my old neighbor came out and started rattling garbage cans. He was really a crazy old guy. He always rattled the garbage cans. And this guy looked up at me, and then he hobbled away. So they didn't get my dollar. And I was able to get my vindication. And I won't leave New York. (M-83)

This story isolates two common themes of the trickster/victim story: being taken by surprise, and quick thinking on the victim's part. The narrator suggests that the criminal picked a wrong target: students are often without money. In the narrative itself, the victim manipulated several stereotypes about criminals for the audience, one being that muggings are motivated solely because of costly drug habits: "I thought, I only have a dollar. . . . That's not enough for a fix." Stopping the assailant worked in this case because the "shrimpy fellow" had met up with a victim twice his size who overpowered him. Few stories have this theme, and in some stories, the victim that shows cunning does not always escape danger.

By and large, most victims resort to giving the offenders the money, rather than putting up a fight with someone who is armed. "Giving in" is seen as a solution rather than a defense. Moreover, most narrators seem to want a resolution of the crime and to know that the offenders might be apprehended. Many times, informants end the story with the appearance of the police. The following narrative, reported second-hand, has several of the trickster themes. Despite the victim's ordeal she thinks quickly on her feet, and helps in the apprehension of the rapist:

Uh, let's see. I was working . . . there about 1973. . . . So it would be like '72, okay? She came in one day all excited and said something about her girlfriend had been raped, or we had been talking about rape at that time. Apparently, her girlfriend was single, living on the East Side somewhere, and . . . two blacks broke into her apartment and proceeded to completely rip off the apartment, and then they raped her. And apparently they also asked her for cash. Well, she had no cash on her. She had about ten dollars. And they said, "You're goin' to be in bad shape if we don't get any kind of money." So she said, "Well, listen, I'll write you out a check." And he said,

"Okay, fine. Write me out a check." And she says, "Do you want me to make it out to cash?" And he says, "No, because if you make it out to cash and I bring it into a bank, nobody will ever cash it for me. So make it out to my name, okay?" And he gave her his name. . . . as soon as they left, she called the cops and says, "Such and such happened, [he] took my apartment apart, raped me. But his name is SO AND SO!" They picked him up in a couple of days. They found the guy. **(R-4)**

The humor of the story contrasts with a vicious rape and ransacking. The victim is depicted as representative of many urban, single women. She lives alone and has a fashionable address, yet she can't escape from crime in New York City, even in the confines of her own home. Though she suffers the attack, she is quick-witted enough to ask for the rapist's name, and he is foolish enough to give her the key to his conviction. The clever victim, in this case, is symbolic of the woman who takes some control of the situation by reporting the rape to the authorities.

The tellers of these stories view the tricksters and offenders as people who prey on the kindnesses and good graces of unsuspecting, law-abiding citizens. Offenders, and even more trickster/offenders, are amoral characters testing the boundaries of the social order. There is always an imbalance of power and a reversal of the characters' status. Victims are quickly placed in subordinate roles once the attack by the offender is made apparent. The offender's display of power infuriates the victims or narrator. "How dare he point a gun at me?" is a common response once the event is over and the victim is free from danger. Victims may resent that they have become an accessory to a social problem, such as the relationship between crime and drugs, or they are angry at what they perceive to be an overwhelming increase in street crime and police indifference and the law enforcers' inability to control it. At times, victims boast of how they got themselves out of a dangerous situation, and their actions often elicit praise and admiration from listeners. What is being praised, however, is the victim's return to his/her initial status and power. Second-hand reporters and listeners identifying with the victim in the story see the clever victim as a projection of themselves. The win for the victim is a win for them. This projection is one reason these clever-victim stories are so well received by listeners. They serve as an outlet for channeling hostility toward offenders.

TRADITIONAL STORIES TOLD AS CRIME-VICTIM NARRATIVES

Several second-hand narratives recorded for this collection can be recognized as versions of other folklore forms. Though cast as crime-victim stories by their tellers, they are adaptations of urban legends, traditional tale plots, stories about the traditional scam—the confidence game—and the shaggy dog story.[26] They show similar features in style and structure to the crime-victim stories and serve similar purposes. Both address human predicaments by showing how people act in times of crisis and danger. In some cases, they reveal how little human ingenuity, character, and responses to such dangers have changed over time.

The process of folklorization shows that other folklore forms, such as urban legends, may serve as models for reconstructing everyday experience.[27] An urban legend, for example, may masquerade as a crime-victim story. This process also indicates that what has been wisely regarded as traditional material by folklore scholars continues to circulate in urban society. The human tendency to use folklore as a shield against the darker side of human nature seems to be flourishing in contemporary society.

As these crime-victim stories were being collected, one incident was recast as a shaggy dog tale, a modern joke type which the narrator introduced as part of his own crime-victim repertory. This type of tale, filled with detail and repetition, characteristically ends with a humorous punch line that reveals the tale's twist, i.e., "The joke is on you."[28] The following tale was embedded into a conversation about crime in New York City. Tom Christiansen, a college professor, told the story shortly after relating how he had foiled the robbery of his car as thieves attempted to steal it from his garage one winter night in 1977. Here is his version of the urbanite's need to intercede in situations where crime can be thwarted:

> Something similar happened to a student of mine which happened to her boyfriend. This girl told me this story about her boyfriend who goes to Duke University. He was at some store buying all packages, and he was paying for some stuff. And he dropped a twenty-dollar bill. The boyfriend said, "Can I have the twenty-dollar bill?" And a man said, "Can you prove it's yours?" And he said, "No, I can't prove it's mine." And the man said, "Well, do you know the serial numbers on it?" And he said, "No, I just dropped it. You saw me drop it." And the man said, "Well, I found it, so it's mine."
>
> The boyfriend went out. He was really mad. He was going to the car, and as he was getting into his car, he had started his car—and he saw the same man coming out of the store. His car was parked right next to his, and he was carrying all these packages. So he put the packages in front of the car. They were all in a big shopping bag. And he started to open the car with a key. And her boyfriend jumped out of his car and grabbed the packages and drove off with the packages. He figured they were his packages. So he got home with the packages. Now the question, What was in the packages? The answer is bologna, like the rest of the story. **(M-39)**

The shaggy dog tale, with its brag ending, which is common to the genre, is not unlike the trickster/clever victim story. Both rely on a twist ending or a trick played on the character within the story. The two narrative types share other similarities, as well. Both are told to infuse a moment of suspense into what at first seems to be an ordinary encounter in a routine day. As with the trickster tale and other crime-victim narratives, the veracity of the story is hardly questioned. In the shaggy dog tale, it is only at the end of the story that the listener realizes that he or she is getting a good leg-pulling and some comic relief to a possibly dangerous, but common, confrontation. The shaggy dog tale is so convincing because, as in the crime-victim story, rude and dehumanizing behavior is recognizable. The familiar nastiness of the store's patrons makes the listener even more gullible. Both stories emphasize the hostility and lack of civility urbanites show one another. Unlike the shaggy dog tale, crime-victim stories have endings that are usually tragic. And most crime-victim characters, perhaps with the exception of the clever victim, would rarely act like the man in the above tale. Most shy away from revenge because of fear.

It is not surprising that informants of first-person narratives and second-hand retellings include some examples of traditional urban lore. For example, informants told stories about the confidence game, or the "pigeon drop," alongside crime-victim stories, making little, if any, distinction between narratives about crime victimization and those about "victimless" crimes without physical danger. In the confidence game, the unsuspecting target is usually approached by two tricksters asking for aid. The first example, told by Bernadette Potter, emphasizes how she was aware of the ruse and refused to be duped, unlike her co-worker, who fell for the scheme:

I was still working in midtown. On my way to the bank on Fifty-seventh Street and Broadway . . . these two people stopped me. Two black people. A black woman and a black man. They had Southern accents. One person came over to me. "Miss, can you help me?" She had an envelope that had some really bad handwriting on it. It was obviously written by someone who didn't know how to address an envelope. So, I was telling her to go to the post office or a policeman, and maybe they could help her. All of a sudden, a man comes over. "Miss, did you ever find the address?" "No, this lady is going to help me." All of a sudden they said, "Let's open it up and see what's in the envelope." That's when something clicked in my head. Then they read this note. "Dear Sam, This is the $10,000 that I owe you from my trip to Las Vegas." No, "my trip to Cuba." That's what it was. "Thanks again, Love, John." That's when I said, "This is shit!" Come on, this is the confidence game! . . . And I just looked at them and said, "Ah, come on!" I think I told them to go to hell, and then I walked away.

Half an hour later, I get back to the office, and everything was in a stir. I said, "You're not going to believe what happened to me!" Then I started to tell them the story of what happened. Elsa walked in five minutes later and said there was this girl who was ripped off in a confidence game. And everybody just froze. I said, "What did they look like?" And she gave a general description. I said, "Of course, they were the same people who accosted me, and they obviously ripped off this girl for fifty bucks." It was her last money or something like that. I called the police, and they acted very nonchalant about it, but they took my description anyway. And that's what happened. I don't know if they were ever caught. That was very weird.[29]

The second example, told by Irene Whitefield, underscores the gullibility of the target:

When I was a kid, the New York World's Fair was in town in 1965. I remember reading a *Life* article . . . about con games you had to watch out for. And now, you know, so many years later it's happening again. I couldn't believe it. It's so old and ridiculous. But a woman that I work with was in Rockefeller Center, and sure enough, this woman came up to her and started doing a routine that is called the "Found Money" game. Somebody says, "Look, I have this problem. I found this envelope, and I don't know who it's for, and it's bothering me. What should I do? Let's see what's inside." So you look inside, and there's a lot of money inside. And she says, "Oh, golly, I think I'd better take this to my boss, please come with me." And eventually you're supposed to either put in part of the money or take it, and eventually they switch it around. I couldn't believe they were trying this on this woman, but they did.[30]

In both stories, the narrators emphasize the gullibility of the victim, and express surprise that con games still continue on urban streets despite warnings against them.[31] A few crime-victim narratives in the collection can be classified as urban legends. Though not all urban legends deal with crime and victimization, several well-known, popular legends do, including "The Hook" and "The Killer in the Backseat."[32] Several narratives told as second-hand crime-victim stories were, on closer scrutiny, urban legends. Both narrative types share some common features, so the adaptability of the urban legend to the crime-victim story should not be all that surprising. For example, both are believed or supposed to be based on true experiences. Urban legends "mistakenly" told as crime-victim stories circulate widely, are localized, and contain traditional plots. Both are told as events that happened to a friend of a friend, and of course, the source of the story is rarely, if ever, verified.

While there are many different urban legends that circulate nationwide, three well-known ones use New York City as their setting.[33] All three deal with victimization or the expectation of violence. In the popular mind, New York City is believed to be crime-ridden, so that view lends plausibility to the legends. Most urban legends circulate to express the fears and anxieties of the majority. In this case, they project a generalized fear of anonymous muggers and of New York City in general. The first is about a jogger in Central Park, the second is about a hurt robber, and a third is about a bus rider.

"The Central Park Jogger" concerns a man taking his usual run through the park when a fellow jogger brushes by him. Incensed, the jogger thinks that the man has stolen his wallet, so he picks up his pace, determined to catch him. He runs up to him, looks him in the eye, and yells: "Give me the wallet!" Frightened, the second jogger quickly hands over a wallet, which the first man puts in his pocket. The first jogger continues his run and heads home. When he arrives there, he finds his own wallet, which he had absent-mindedly left on his bureau. Thinking that he was the victim of a crime, he finds that he himself has committed one. Esther Silverman, whose other crime-victim stories have been previously cited, was convinced that the incident was true:

> Yes, I've heard that story, but it's been going around for a while. I heard that they thought he stole his wallet. And he ran after him, and he beat him up, and he took his wallet. And when he got home, he found that he had two wallets. **(M-82)**

This popular urban legend was circulating at a time when running fever had gripped the city. It is actually a modern, or current, variant of an urban legend collected by Katherine Briggs in 1912, and used by Neil Simon in the film version of *The Prisoner of Second Avenue*.[34] Known as "The Five Pound Note" in Briggs's collection *The Folktales of England,* the story is about a woman who goes into town to do some shopping. Her brother gives her a five-pound note to spend. On the train, she sits next to a woman who dozes off. When the shopper happens to open her purse, she sees that her five-pound note is missing. She then looks in the woman's purse, and sees a five-pound note on the top of her belongings. She pockets it and silently accuses the woman of stealing it. When she returns home, the woman is surprised when her brother asks her how she could have purchased anything in town, since she had left the five-pound note at home.[35]

The similarity between the two legends is obvious, but there is one substantial difference. While both falsely accuse a stranger of theft, in the Briggs version the woman clearly expresses concern and remorse for her action. " 'Old scoundrel,' thought Mrs. M. . . . 'She's poor and old, and I oughtn't to have put temptation in her way.' She wondered what she ought to do. It would cause a great deal of delay and bother to call the police, and it seemed cruel to get an old woman into trouble, but she must have her money."[36] In the urban legend about the man in Central Park, in contrast, neither the jogger nor the teller exhibits any remorse about the mugging.

In fact, the mugger's actions are regarded as right. Certain that the other jogger mugged him, he indignantly—even bravely—asks for his wallet. No remorse over stealing or even "restealing" one's own money is shown. Central Park is, after all, a mugger's haven, and the act of asking for the wallet back seems almost noble. Though a listener might wonder what story the victim has to tell, the humor and the case of mistaken identity—actually human fraility and suspicion—give the legend the ingredients needed for it to be remembered.

A social worker, Susan Roberts from Brooklyn, narrated several stories about her clients who met weekly in a neighborhood agency. One story in particular sounded like an urban legend. It was told as a second-hand report of a crime-victim incident that Roberts insisted was true:

> She's a very articulate woman—when she went blind four years ago, she really got herself together. She's very independent—she's totally blind, but she is mobile. She gets around, does what she has to do. She went through a bad depression, except nothing stops her. She took mobility training, and she's independently strong—very wonderful woman. And she's really a kind, generous woman. She went home from the agency, and then the doorbell rang. And she has a chain on her door, and she just opened the door. Someone said it was a messenger or something, and she didn't really question it. She opened the door—this guy grabbed her entire arm and took sandpaper and just started scratching her entire arm up and down. And he told her to break the chain or he's gonna ruin her arm with this sandpaper. And she just tried as much as she could not to present herself as a victim, you know, the idea that you can't be hurt, or that you can't be treated as a victim if you don't present yourself like a victim. So what she did was she grabbed the guy's arm and said, "You have no right treating me like this! Who the hell do you think you are?" She grabbed his hand, and with all her energy she took his fingers with all her strength and broke them all—all his fingers broke like spaghetti. And he ran off. She called the cops. And they picked him up a few hours later because he went to an emergency room in a hospital because he had five broken fingers. She refused to be a victim. (M-9)

As with many urban legends accounts, the teller never questioned how someone could be fatally hurt by sandpaper. Nevertheless, the teller believed the narrative to be true and could clearly identify the victim. It is difficult to tell how the story was embellished, or whether it took the features of the well-known urban legend of "The Robber Who Was Hurt." In this urban legend, well documented by Jacquelyn Simpson and Jan Brunvand, a robber breaks into a woman's apartment.[37] In attempting to defend herself, the frightened woman picks up a hot fireplace poker and burns the intruder. He immediately leaves, and she runs downstairs to tell a neighbor about the incident. The neighbor is upset herself, because her husband has just come home with a severe burn. As in the narrative about the blind woman, the offender is identified by the assault brought on by the intended victim's act of self-protection. This brings to mind the crime-victim story told by Bernadette, who marked the rapist's heel with a knife, resulting in his identification by the police hours later, or the story of the rapist who cashed his victim's check.

Sociologist Lyn Lofland points out that in today's urban society, it is difficult to differentiate between the Good Samaritans and the harm-doers.[38] Clearly this is a message of the crime-victim stories that are disguised as legends, and particularly that of the Central Park jogger who assumes that anyone approaching him intends to do harm. The hurt robber legend warns listeners to be suspicious of those at the door. Both legends reinforce a theme discussed earlier: always suspect danger.

City stories many times use public transportation scenes or the difficulty of getting from one place to another quickly as a motif. For example, a transportation strike can set the city into near-panic; muffled radio traffic reports can create confusion, as can gridlock street conditions. Motorists continually tell stories about the rude driving habits of others, the battles in traffic court, the ruthless meter maids, or the day their car was towed for illegal parking. Urbanites also talk about their experiences with subways and buses, for these are two places where victimization is expected. In several stories, the subway is the scene of the crime.

It is not surprising that legends, or threads of legend plots, or even their settings form the kernel of some of these crime-victim stories, since both reflect a human response to a threatening situation. Since events are set in places of public transportation—the subway car or the bus—it seems credible that violent incidents could occur.

Following is a legend that has circulated in New York City for some time, though it has not been documented in the folk literature. Again, this story was considered true by the informants and was told as a crime-victim story; but it is actually a popular urban legend. The legend is about a man on a bus. He is wearing a trenchcoat, and the sleeves are so long that his hands are nearly covered. Because the bus is overcrowded, he is shoved by a nearby passenger. Suddenly, a woman's bloodied hand, jewelry on its mutilated fingers intact, falls to the floor. The passengers are horrified.[39] This legend, like the crime-victim stories, highlights or under-scores the possibilities of witnessing or being party to a crime. Below are two crime-victim narratives that bear a striking similarity to the legend mentioned above:

> I've witnessed chain rip-offs. I've seen a lot of them. That's when someone pulls a gold chain off someone's neck and runs off. This was about a month ago on the subway. I see these two guys. They were looking around for trouble. You could tell. They were looking around. There was a woman near

the door on that subway. And I wanted to warn her, but they were watching me, too. They were watching me watch her. I was too scared to say anything like, close your jacket. Atlantic Avenue came. And they got the chain and ran off. And she was screaming. And that was it. They just rip it and leave and run. I was feeling real helpless. I could see they were up to no good. (M-76)

Clara Gold, who knew of the above incident, narrated the following one:

There's the one that horrified everyone, of course, the one out in Astoria of the woman wearing a very large Greek cross. You didn't hear that one? This is something. I heard about it, and I read about it in the paper, but it has gone around. People are discussing it. A woman was wearing a large Greek cross, which means that there are two crossbars—gold with rubies. Somebody tried to grab it off her neck . . . the latest refinement on "Let's Snatch the Chain"—you drive up in a car next to someone crossing the street and you rip it, and then the person guns the engine. In this case, they opened the door; the guy was on the passenger side. He grabbed the chain. But the chain itself was not gold, and it was a gold alloy, and it wasn't soft enough to break, and they dragged the woman for a block and a half. . . . Her head kept banging into different cars. Oh, yeah, she died. They got the guys, too. (M-71)

These three examples of legends told as crime stories, and crime-victim stories that have a legendlike flavor and content, are interesting for several reasons. First, they show a transformation of content from one genre to another and a malleability between forms. Second, they show the possibility that crime-victim incidents are actually the basis, or origin, for unexplainable, crime-centered urban legends. Third, the crime-victim stories indicate how stories are cast into the wider net of urban legends, both explaining a human response to a feature of modern urban life.

As demonstrated in this chapter, crime-victim narratives have repeatable themes, content, and character types that continually resurface. Their repetition lends evidence to the argument that these stories constitute a subgenre of the personal-experience narrative. Because of a lack of corroborative research on the folklore of crime, it is difficult to establish the derivation of the content of the stories using a systematic and conventional method common to folklore study. As a result, comparisons between these narratives for their themes and characters and parallels in folk tradition have revealed that these crime-victim stories bear the stamp of folklore from the urban world.

CHAPTER THREE

The Traditional Style of the Crime-Victim Narrative

Violence is one of humankind's oldest story themes, dating back to the early epics. Common to the American cultural heritage and to its folk tradition are narratives that emphasize not only violence but criminal behavior—tall tales of Wild West shootouts, ballads about criminals' last farewells, legends of horrific murders, and sagas about notorious outlaws, for example.[1] This focus on crime and violence continues in contemporary oral tradition. Today, information about serial murderers wanted by the FBI, repeat offenders, or crime victims can be found in every metropolitan American newspaper. Folklore about crime may seem ubiquitous, but what appears to be a contemporary fascination with such stories is actually part of a long-standing and distinctive American tradition.[2]

Human adventure is at the heart of all narrative expression. How these experiences are channeled into a creative outlet such as storytelling is certainly a puzzle for folklorists. Contemporary folklorists no longer question that storytelling is a social activity. Stories are shared because they are pleasurable to hear, and enable both narrators and audience to achieve distance from the everyday world, a world filled with hardship, frustration, and anxiety. For example, humorous tales allow us to separate ourselves from our own foibles and fallibilities and to laugh at them. One of life's greatest pleasures is to be able to entertain others and to be entertained in turn. But stories about personal experiences also provide information about cultural and social rules for living. In the folk tradition, narrators who tell personal-experience stories, or participate in enacting other folklore forms, usually work within a specific framework. Because they may choose words, phrases, diction, formulae, and performance styles, the mode of presentation is their own. However, narrators are conditioned by and restricted to what is traditionally accepted within their own culture.

A text or story can become traditionalized in one of two ways: by folk cultural material that is handed down by word of mouth, and by the oral replication of a text identifiable by its distinctive stylistic features and structure.[3]

A newly discovered group of texts that have a distinctive, recognizable, and repeatable structure and characteristics, and are traditional to a particular milieu may constitute a new genre of folklore. Here the term *genre* is used to denote a classification in which the features of style and structure for the crime-victim narrative are analyzed. The dramatic and narrative qualities that traditionalize the crime-victim story raise an important question. How does a contemporary story, specifically the crime-victim narrative, become traditionalized? What features of style and structure characterize these urban personal-experience stories as traditional?[4]

Crime-victim narratives have several stylistic features that provide a dramatic structure and resolution. These stories are characterized by step-by-step action leading to the resolution. The insertion of role-playing dialogue between the characters, the lack of repetition of narrative scenes (a singular departure from the pattern of much traditional material), and the emphasis on details important to the plot and narrative asides are typical features. Like the urban legend, the crime-victim narrative is told for truth (though it differs from newspaper accounts about crime); characterization is limited, and the setting is the real world, not the world of fiction.

TRADITIONAL FEATURES

General Characteristics

The crime-victim narrative centers around conflict between two or more people, usually strangers. The stories are most often told as singular episodes in a string of recounted personal narratives about city life. Crime-victim stories are intensely dramatic. They draw attention to the immediate situation of the moment in the story frame. Consequently, they catch the listener's attention right from the start. The narrator usually begins with the time and place of the event. A conflict arises and is resolved, most often with the offender fleeing the scene of the crime, although occasionally the victim calls the police. A coda, ending the story, often suggests certain attitudes towards life in New York City or about crime in general. A declaration of faith in people may be expressed, such as when a stranger helps a wounded victim, but more often a cry of frustration about urban life ends the story. Just the mere threat of violence or the perception of its potential may create the dramatic tension within the narrative. Narrative content and dramatic delivery add tension to the story, as well.

Crime-victim stories rarely contain graphic descriptions of violence, as are frequently found in other forms of American folklore.[5] Though it is presumed that violence characterizes the stories, the violence is sanitized. Few lengthy depictions of physical harm or abuse appear; however, when present, violence is frequently denoted by action verbs as *shoot, kick, beat, hit,* or *jump.* These words are often said in a matter-of-fact tone. Depicting graphic scenes of gratuitous violence is not the main purpose in relating these stories. Nor is violence celebrated as a means to an end. For the victim and for the tellers, survival and perseverance are more important qualities.

The Steady Progression of Action: Synchronic Time

The crime-victim story develops similarly to other oral narratives: by repetition and a recognition of a story-building structure. Crime-victim stories do not have repeated narrative sections or patterned sequences of threefold repetition as do traditional folk narratives. But these stories do have openers, like the folk tale's opening formula of "Once upon a time."[6] For example, a teller might say, "Here's one I've heard," or enter narrative competition with, "Oh I can top that one!" or "I've got a better one." These openers imply that similar events have already been heard, and that tellers and audiences know about them; and, more important, that stories of this type will be heard in the future. After all, city life is commonly defined by these narratives.

The plot of the crime-victim story unfolds logically, following a steady path of action. It can therefore develop quickly, satisfying the listener's curiosity about what happens to the characters. The teller is not overly concerned with the criminal's motivation per se, or even with his or her techniques, though both are essential to the development of the story. It is the resolution of the conflict and the unfolding of how the victim survived that are crucial. The victim's fate is the key to the dramatic quality of the story. Because of an identification with the victim, even the most poorly told yet clearly vicious story seems to be remembered.

The crime-victim story begins with little introduction to the event itself or to its characters. The narratives themselves might be used as conversational icebreakers. This is because tellers and audience share a common frame of reference. They assume that there is no escape from crime in the city world. Thus, lengthy preliminaries are not necessary, except for outsiders, newcomers to New York City. As the story begins, listeners are not provided with clues about what happens to the victim, or the events that lead up to the incident. Sometimes, the individual characters are familiar; the victim and the narrator are often one and the same. But victims in these stories can also be strangers. Consequently, biographical details are few. In an Aristotelian way, personalities are revealed by action within the story.

Action is essential to the progression of the plot. Background details are insignificant. In fact, excessive detail would only hinder the narrative's flow. Because of the insistence upon "what happened next," the story's dramatic themes are implicitly revealed. As the story unfolds, familiar themes surface. These might include the offender's boldness or audacity, the offender's exercise of power, the threat to life, the physical danger to the victim, the victim's panic or fear, the loss of property, and the violation of personal space.

After reminding the audience that the story can be one of a probable string of stories about urban life, the narrator focuses immediately on the location of the incident, grounding it in time and space and establishing its veracity. In effect, the world of the story becomes real, having recognizable and familiar places and scenes—for example, the New York City Public Library (M-54), Morningside Park (M-17), or Manhattan's Upper West Side (M-53). Once the teller thus "localizes" or personalizes the environment, he or she focuses on the chain of events that lead to a resolution. For example, when Stanley Wolman told a story about his grandmother, he was responding to my question of whether he had heard of anyone being mugged. First he said, "I'm sure I've heard some stories." Then, pausing, he recalled a specific incident. He exclaimed, "Oh, yeah, my aunt has a loft on West Seventeenth Street. My grandmother comes over a lot. She comes over to see them once in a while . . ." (M-5). But immediately after his short "introduction," Wolman locates the core of the story. His grandmother had been tied up and locked in a basement closet by two intruders and was later discovered by his aunt. Few details about the grandmother are presented in the story, but the listeners and perhaps Wolman himself now ascribe a new identity to her—crime victim. He begins by relating the place and time of the event, provides the scantiest of details about his relatives, then emphasizes the most important part of the story—that his grandmother made it through the ordeal. Her survival serves as resolution to the story.

The characters themselves, whether victims or bystanders, have no fully developed qualities or personalities. In another example, Marcia Bobson reports the place and the time of an incident. Like other narrators of these stories, she tells little about what she was doing right beforehand. She reports that she was walking down a Manhattan street when several "guys" harassed her, and one attempted to molest her. She said anxiously, "I was walking crosstown on Fifty-seventh Street East, and I was right on 250 West Fifty-seventh Street. There were some guys taking stuff into a building, and it looked like a delivery." Marcia continued, "And before I knew what was happening, he was molesting me." She resisted and swung back, smacking the man on his ear with her purse. She then fled to her apartment a few blocks away, immediately telling her husband what had happened. During our interview, Marcia mentioned that even though they had lived in Chicago for several years, nothing like this unprovoked attack had ever before happened to her. Here again, in Marcia's story, the focus is on the action—we aren't given a clue to why she was on that street in the first place, or whether any other event precipitated the incident. She did mention to me during our interview that she began carrying a can of condensed soup in her purse for several months after the incident to "thwart" anyone who would dare to approach her again (**M-40).**

Victims, and even witnesses, have surprising stories to tell. For example, one summer evening, Ellen Schwartz witnessed a violent rape from her bedroom window. "Then there is the thing that happened across the street from me. Last July, the end of July. It was almost a year ago." She paused and then continued, "I think it was July twenty-third." She nodded her approval at her precise recall of detail, as she spoke into my tape recorder in an Upper West Side luncheonette.[7] "It was four-thirty in the morning," she continued **(R-9).** As she spoke, she unfolded a lengthy, horrifying account of a man who attacked and then attempted to rape a neighbor after breaking into her second-floor apartment. He entered through an open window, boosting himself up onto a garbage can. The night was hot, a New York scorcher. The woman had left the window open for some air. The man had been seen lurking around the neighborhood. Ellen herself had seen him and even had complained once or twice about him to the police. On that eventful summer night, Ellen just couldn't sleep. Absent-mindedly, she glanced out of her window and witnessed the surprising scene. At first, she was unclear about what was going on. "And I said to myself, 'Hold on, now, you're too liberal; just because he is fully dressed and she is in her nightgown and he is beating the shit out of her doesn't mean that they don't know each other and they don't like it that way.' I mean, you just can't scream rape at four o'clock in the morning in New York." But then she realized that the woman was in distress. Ellen leaned out of her window and screamed across the early dawn street to her: "Is everything all right?" She put the police whistle she was holding in her hand into her mouth, blew it loudly, and alerted the neighborhood: "STOP RAPIST!" she hollered. Discovered, the man leapt off the now half-clad woman, slipped out the apartment window, and fled down the street. A few minutes later, the battered and bruised victim was in Ellen's apartment talking with the police and thanking her for intervening. Ellen was to learn later that the precinct switchboard had "lit up like a Christmas tree" because of her cry of alarm.

Such stories are set in common urban places—apartment lobbies, elevators, vestibules, subways, buses, the open street. The locales provide another way to highlight the story action. But because the settings are so ordinary, victims and nonvictims, narrators and listeners, are apt to reevaluate their environments after an incident occurs. Ellen, for example, wondered if she should move from her now "dangerous" neighborhood to a "safer" one.[8] Precisely because the events of the stories occur in such common places, these settings suddenly become the scene for everyday drama. The elevator becomes the danger room, the city street the murder place, the subway car the den of thieves.

The Central Characters

Crime-victim narratives generally have three main characters: the victim (hero/heroine), the offender (villain), and the occasional witnesses or bystanders to the scene. The victim and the bystanders are inert characters; though they might act heroically, they are not heroes or heroines in the true sense. The victim is acted upon, and the bystanders, when they do appear, watch the action. It is the offender who provokes the action and is the most active of the characters.

Because the primary intention of the narrator is to get to the resolution of the story, he or she lingers only on significant details or actions, since an impatient audience might wonder about the victim's fate, and consequently the teller would lose their attention. As a result, the characters in these stories of modern life are one-dimensional and lack development. As with the common characters of the urban legend, their personality traits are superficial. For example, the victims in urban legends are often foolish or naive. In the crime-victim story, the victims are not only naive but also frightened, vulnerable, and at times unusually trusting of others. They are unaware of the dangers surrounding them. We never see them as rounded, complex people who are motivated by psychological reasoning. They never seem to wonder why urban crime exists, or how the crime rate can be decreased, or what the consequences and costs of crime are to society. The victim characters in these stories are caricatures of urban life—the common person of the city street. For the most part, they represent relatives, friends, acquaintances, and coworkers, i.e., our social network. But the characters need to be abstractions, because the intention of most narrators is to bring the conflict to its conclusion as swiftly as possible and arrive at the coda—the point of the story. For example, the English teacher who was robbed at gunpoint in front of her students is unfortunately less significant to the audience as an individual victim than as a symbol of the decline of discipline and the increase of violence in inner-city schools.

Like the victims, the bystanders are inert characters. They simply witness the conflict, rarely intervening to rescue the victim from harm. Their function is to represent the apathetic citizen, common in urban stories. While bystanders play a benign role in the stories, they are usually criticized by the listeners, who expect or wish them to help the victim. In several stories, the bystanders are policemen. Their appearance often prompts a listener to say, "Where is a cop when you need one?"

The offenders, or villains, in the story are the most active of the three central characters. Along with victims and bystanders, they are described quickly in bland terms. In most of the stories I collected, the alleged offender is a young black male. He may be "just a guy," or a "black kid," or a "young black dude."[9] Such standard designations are particularly powerful, because in several cases the narrators stereotype these characters by assuming they are offenders with past criminal records. Common terms such as "a black kid" or "a young black dude" are often synonymous with racial slurs, equating young black males with persistent troublemakers. The offender isn't around long enough to make a personal impression. The victim has a more lasting impression of the incident itself than of the figures involved in it. Occasionally, offenders are identified by occupational labels: the security guard, the elevator operator, the policeman. But they still remain one-dimensional characters. Thus, the emphasis is less on the relationship between the characters than on the action between them.

Emphasis on the Climactic Scene and the Economy of Suspense

Crime-victim stories seem purposely short and staccato—quickly charged, urban, and fast-paced—resembling life in the city in which they are set. Like the urban motorist who wants to get from one place to another in the shortest time using the most lightly traveled streets, these stories have few detours.

Soon after the abstract characters are introduced, the teller comes to the story's most powerful moment: the confrontation between the soon-to-be-victim and the perpetrator of the crime. When the story first begins, only the narrator knows the outcome—whether the victim will live or die, whether the offender will be captured or flee. The audience has only a few clues as to the story's direction. The interest lies in how the narrator creates suspense for effect and how it is used to bring the audience into the circle. For example, when Bernadette crosses the busy street to get the key to return home, we have little idea of the rape scene that will be shortly presented. When a Brooklyn woman returns home from vacation and is met by a "friendly stranger" who helps her to her door, we have no clue that he will later assault her. The audience has been brought into the story much as a bystander would be. In the climactic scenes, the offender and the victim may negotiate. The victim might try to humor the offender or pretend to misinterpret his directions or the seriousness of the situation; however, this attempt to thwart victimization is not always successful.

As a bystander to the unfolding of the plot, the listener is caught up in a sense of intrigue similar to that evoked by reading a good murder mystery. Of course, the plots of crime-victim stories are simple to follow and certainly less convoluted than those of many mystery stories or television detective shows. Nevertheless, the listener is intrigued by the story, and is both curious and often gullible. At first, he or she is an unwitting participant—"Oh, this could never happen to me!" Yet as the story continues and the setting and situation seem more common, listeners are transported into the victim's world, realizing when the climactic scenes are reached that such things could indeed happen to them. The identification with the victim is one reason that these stories about urban life are so popular. The audience's identification, at first negligible, becomes stronger by the story's end. Although the roles of each character are not clear at the beginning of the story, they are clarified quickly. Sides are taken. Themes in the story that are defined as "incidents" at the beginning unfold as stylized tales by their conclusion.

Narrative Asides

Asides are a common feature in oral narratives, and they figure widely into these personal-experience stories. The purpose of this device is to call attention to the events within the narrative, and to further elaborate on its point. Crime-victim stories include four uses of narrative asides. For example, a narrator might embroider a story, evaluating or commenting on his or her role as the victim in the story; however, these comments break the narrative flow and appear outside of the story. Often, narrators comment on how the story events affected them: "I never thought this could happen to me." In another type of narrative aside, the narrator evaluates how others acted in the victim situation. This type of aside also stops the flow of the story.[10]

> This happened a couple of years ago. There was a teacher at my school. . . .
> She wasn't teaching there. It was his wife. I think she was at home, and
> somebody came into her apartment and wanted to rob it. He found her at
> home, and he got scared. And instead of just running, he beat her to death.
> And the husband found her in a pool of blood. . . . He found her just like
> that. That freaks me out, because that's someone that I know. I know
> him. . . . this happened when I first started to teach in the school, and we
> got along with each other pretty well. And they were so happily married.
> Real together. They never got the guy. **(MR-6)**

The above story clearly indicates the use of narrative asides. The narrator, Mary Simmons, implies how vicious the offender was, but she comments primarily on her association with the victim's husband and how that association affected her. Like most other narrators, she embeds the asides into the story. Narrative asides rarely appear as openers, since listeners need a frame of reference to understand why the teller needs or wants to make the point. As in Simmons's story, this device is frequently used to suspend the story's action. Furthermore, the aside appears right before the coda: "They never got the guy."

In these stories, one of the most common types of narrative aside is internal: the frequent use of dramatized dialogue within a story. In the traditional ballad, a story told in song, dialogue is often the vehicle that reveals the conflict between the principal characters.[11] Urban legends—contemporary stories about unusual or unexplainable events, such as finding a mouse in your coke, or dipping into a bucket of fried chicken and coming up with a rat instead of a drumstick—often use dialogue to add verisimilitude, as "evidence" that the event in question could indeed have happened. Like the ballad and the urban legend, the folktale also uses dialogue to make the characters of the fictional world come to life, and to have the hero solve his dilemma through interactions with the story characters. All such forms of folklore, particularly the ballad, use dialogue to slow down and focus on the story line. In the crime-victim story, dialogue is used in the same way. It provides the stage for the subsequent resolution—whether or not the character victim survives the event.

Using dialogue in a "true story" is another way in which the narrator, eyewitness, or victim, or even second- or third-hand reporters, can "claim" the story. Tellers can also inject their own personal style into these accounts.[12] They can speed up the narration to a dramatic point and infuse it with a sense of immediacy and action. Or they can incorporate New Yorkisms into their stories by using common colloquial expressions such as "like," "you know," and "ya know what I mean?" to extend the action. Like other narrators, they can use their voices to instill a sense of fear, use facial mannerisms to express excitement, surprise, or horror, or use hand gestures or body posture to act out the story. A good storyteller is often a good actor. For example, Irene Whitefield role-played each character when relating her story. She showed me how she grabbed a man's hand while he was dipping his fingers into the purse of the woman in front of him, as he and his victim were going around in the revolving door of the New York City Public Library (**M-54**). Dialogue enables the teller to create a brief urban drama. It conveys a certain perspective on urban reality, telling the audience what the reporter believes to have happened. Because these events are so often spoken, their components are a part of a traditional urban folk conversation. Dialogue gives the story some punch, infusing it with a sense that "you are there." Dialogue can often add a comic touch to the dramatic scene, especially when the tension is high and has been sustained for several minutes.

In these stories, the teller prepares others for what they might expect in a time of crisis. It is interesting that even when there is no face-to-face interaction between a victim and an offender within the story scene, reporters might fashion conversations between other characters who could be involved in the event. Informants did tell me stories about house robberies that are not included in this collection; however, in telling, the informants created conversation—for example, a dialogue between a victim and a locksmith changing locks on a newly burgarized apartment might be included in the story.

Here's an example of how dialogue is used as an aside and is deftly incorporated into a story. One late evening, Joe Bowers, an actor living in New York City, was heading home. He was walking down East Eleventh Street off Fifth Avenue in Greenwich Village to the subway. He had just spent a quiet evening with a friend watching television. "I was just walking down the street going to the IRT subway to catch my train to go home. I was walking down the street. . . . I was kind of watching the sidewalk, because you have to in New York," he chuckled, and then cupped his palm over his mouth and giggled nervously. "Anyway, so I was walking down the street, and I wasn't paying attention to what was going on around me." Joe noticed a man walking toward him on the same side of the street. To avoid a collision, Joe sidestepped left.[13] "All of a sudden," Joe continued, "he jumped in front of me into my path." Looking menacing and vicious, the man held a club up over Joe's head. Then, with his other hand, he pointed a knife at his belly. He now towered over Joe, a mere five-foot-five. The armed man spoke: "Don't say anything, just give me your money." Frightened, Joe replied to him, "Sure, here." Joe reached down into his pocket and handed over a few dollars. Still not satisfied by the meager haul, the threatening man shouted another demand, "Give me all of it!" "Sure," said Joe after digging into his pocket and then slapping some pennies into the man's hand. "There it is, that's everything." But the greedy man demanded more: "Give me your watch!" Joe again acquiesced: "Here, sure. There you go." The offender, finally satisfied, started to run down the street. He turned and yelled out one more demand: "All right, now just keep going and don't look back." At first, Joe was a bit stunned, since the incident happened so quickly. Then he curtly said to the man, "Okay, goodnight." He then bolted for the subway stop, clutching a saved subway token in his hand. "I wanted to get home," he explained. (M-19).

This example contains many of the essential elements of the classic crime-victim narrative. Joe meets the stranger after dark on an otherwise well-traveled Manhattan street. At first, he is almost undaunted by the situation, as suggested by the blasé tone he uses to tell his story. "Sure, here it is," he says when he gives in to the demands of the man. His delivery of the deadpan dialogue is almost casual. Joe is the jaded New Yorker par excellence. His cynicism and nonchalance conceal how frightened he is by the experience. His perfectly controlled actions underscore a common folk attitude: it's only a matter of time before they get you!

The Attention to Particular Detail

Everyone likes a good story, especially a cliffhanger. One of the purposes of these crime-victim stories about city life is to enthrall and even scare the listeners, filling them with a momentary fear and uneasiness about life in New York City. To a large degree, these modern tales are replacements for the ghost stories and other scary tales that were once popularly told to amuse, frighten, and titillate.[14]

To create this mood of suspense and momentary danger, some narrators pay particular attention to details within the story frame, exaggerating some while eliminating others. For example, as we have just seen, through the use of dialogue, a teller can show off a flair for the dramatic. He or she may pause, take a breath, change the tone of voice, and/or incorporate gestures, all contributing to the resolution of the story. As with other traditional narratives, details that seem insignificant to the plot often change or are pared away after successive renditions, while other small details become significant. A story about an elderly couple who were beaten and robbed in their Brooklyn home one Saturday afternoon several years ago serves as an example of how details are important to the style of the crime-victim story.

"The Apartment Sale" was told by Ruth Melberg in her Brooklyn home. Once a medical secretary, Ruth was nearly sixty years old and was disabled at the time of our sessions. She passed the time with her friends and neighbors by playing card games, gossiping, and telling stories.[15] She was known among them as a good storyteller, and she would often hold forth. If interrupted, she would add such comments as, "Let me finish," or "Let me go on," or "Come on, let me tell you what happened." Some of her stories could last for close to thirty or forty minutes. Her narrative style is best described as "urban-combative" and aggressive. She wouldn't hesitate to say that New York City "just isn't what it used to be when you could go out on the streets at all hours of the night and day and not need to worry."

Ruth's story involved a retired couple who decided to hold a sort of urban garage sale in their apartment before relocating to a Florida condominium. They placed an advertisement in a New York newspaper. After one successful weekend, they had still more items to sell, and decided to hold a second sale. But Ruth warned them not to hold either one. Ruth said, "I warned them not to do it because I told them you don't know who was coming into your house." But the trusting couple ignored her warning and claimed that nothing bad could possibly happen. During the second Saturday sale, many people sauntered in and out of their home throughout the day. Around midafternoon, two buyers, a man and his son, appeared. They seemed interested in some of the merchandise. "How much would it be?" asked the father, pointing at an item. Ruth's friends told him. The father claimed that he didn't have enough cash for the items and asked the seller, Jesse, if they could return for them later in the day. Jesse asked him what time he could expect his return, since he and his wife, Julia, had made dinner plans for 6:00 P.M. "Oh, I'll be back before then," said the father. And so the two made a deal, and Jesse put the items aside, assuming the sale was made.

At five-thirty the man and his son showed up as promised and met Jesse in his apartment. Just before their dinner appointment, Julia, Jesse's wife, left the apartment to wait on the street for their dinner companions, who were expected at six o'clock. Time passed, and the three waited anxiously for Jesse to join them, but he did not appear. "So she decided to go up and call him." Ruth paused. She took a deep breath and went on, straightening up in her chair, puffing furiously on a Marlboro. "So," she said slowly, "she goes upstairs to her floor, and she puts the key in the door, and just as she opened the door, her husband yells, 'Julia, don't come in here, they're holding me up!'" Ruth, with a look of fright on her face, then said, "She sees her husband with a terrible gash over his forehead." The man and his son bound the couple, gathered their goods, opened the door, and slipped out of the building without being noticed by anyone. Ruth's suspicion foreshadowed the moment of danger: her warning was ignored, and the violent encounter was the result. The couple were found by their friends, and the police were called, but according to Ruth, the man and his son were never apprehended. Ruth concluded: "That was another incident of people being fooled by letting strangers into their house." Though her final comment is a summation of the story, it is the importance of the details (the buyers' return, the dinner hour, the wife's return) that adds to the story's suspense.

Resolutions and Codas

Crime-victim narratives have three common and identifiable resolutions. An offender may flee the scene, like the rapist who fled from the apartment-building laundry room after confronting a potential victim (**R-6**). Or the victim may sneak away from his or her pursuers, as Irene Whitefield did the time she suddenly turned onto another street when being followed.[16] (**M-49**). Or the teller may conclude the story by mentioning that the police have been called in to intervene. The story will end abruptly as if both the narrator and the listeners expect the police to "set the scene right." Narrators are concerned about whether the offender was apprehended or if he got off "scot-free." "They never found out who did it," or "They never caught the guy" reiterates the teller's vision of the city: a place where victims are preyed upon by violent urban bogeymen who are still out there.

Once the story reaches its conclusion, the teller will comment about the victim's emotional or physical state. This discussion of the aftermath or trauma of the event is another traditional ending to the story, and its most common resolution. Tellers show sympathy for the victim, for after all, the story's purpose is to illustrate the victim's situation. A typical statement might be, "He was very close to being killed. It's incredible." **(M-43)**, or "She couldn't scream. She couldn't do anything. She was just so scared" **(M-78)**. Narrators insist on having resolutions and codas to their stories because of a human, psychological need for closure. The codas prompt the teller and the audience to reflect upon the circumstances within the story. Some change their daily behavior because of the discussed event, avoiding a particular street or neighborhood, or learning new crime-prevention techniques and incorporating them into daily routines. Some of the common codas express predictability: "Where else but New York could this happen?" or "That's the end," or "Isn't it a shame!" or "You just are not safe anywhere these days" **(M-65)**.

The Structure of the Crime-Victim Narrative

All the narratives in the Appendix were labeled as crime-victim stories by the informants, regardless of their length. The meaning of the story does not depend on its length, structure, or stylistic features. However, as I listened to story after story, hour after hour, and analyzed the accounts in depth, it became apparent that in addition to the features described, the crime-victim narrative has a predictable pattern or structure similar to that of other forms of folklore. These stories are composed of seven identifiable units. Some of the narratives in the Appendix contain all seven units; others do not. For example, a narrator may omit a structural unit while telling a story, and continue to its coda without referring to earlier sections of the story. In other words, units are sometimes skipped, but not returned to and added later on. Some stories are longer than others; some are rather short and straight to the point. Outlined below are these seven common structural units of the crime-victim narrative.

I. Establishment of Incident
Crime-Victim Story Introduced by Narrator
   1. Characters within the story are introduced.
      (Type of conflict introduced—optional)
(recursive){ 2. The time of the incident is announced.
            3. The specific place or locale of the incident is cited.

II. Development of Action
   4. Confrontation between the victim and the offender is established. Bystanders are introduced.

5. Simulated dialogue and/or negotiation, exchange of goods occurs between the victim and the offender (or details of robbery surmised). (Use of narrative asides)

III. Resolution of Crime-Victim Event
6. Incident is resolved by characters, and outcome is revealed.

IV. Coda
7. Story concludes with a coda in the form of a rhetorical question, or an evaluation about victim or urban life.

No doubt, these stories are highly predictable. To elucidate their structure, the example below has been plugged into the narrative framework. The story was collected from Bernadette Potter in July, 1977, and tells of a friend who was robbed in the least likely place in New York City—John Jay College of Criminal Justice.[17]

My friend Beverly [crime victim introduced; character within narrative announced] was mugged in the Police Academy, you know, on Jay Street. John Jay College of Criminal Justice [type of conflict/location of incident]. Yeah! In the lobby of the building. Well, that's balls! [narrative aside]. It seems that whoever is supposed to watch people as they come in and out— the guard—wasn't doing his job, and he got fired after that. Well, it seems that this bunch of kids came in, and they stopped her and one of her friends [confrontation between victim and offender; bystander introduced]. So Beverly was saying, "What are you? Crazy? We are all students here. We don't have any money. Don't you know what building this is?" [dialogue] The people who robbed them didn't know where they were and took their money. Okay, whatever money they had. They only had a couple of bucks. How many students have money? [exchange] They said, "Hey, man, you must be kidding. We ain't in there." "Yes, you are!" [said Beverly] "Let's get the hell out of here!" [said the muggers] One of the people had gone up and robbed one of the professors in the building [resolution]. Which goes to show you, where are you safe these days? [coda] **(M-21)**

Diagramming Bernadette's narrative points out how features of style and structure are integrated and suggests that style enhances the structure. Both the particular structure of the story and its stylistic features provide the traditional framework, the flesh and bones, of these narratives. This combination of qualities "traditionalizes" these folk narratives.

TRADITIONAL NARRATIVE STRATEGIES

So far, several features that describe the stylization that occurs in the telling of the crime-victim narrative and its common structure have been examined. The strategies that narrators use to tell these crime-victim stories will now be discussed. These include the use of asides embedded in the narrative, inference and implication to draw attention to the narrative details within the story, and deduction to sketch in the details of the story that would otherwise be lost. These common strategies play an important role in elucidating the crucial differences between an oral crime-victim story and one that appears in print.

The Incorporation of Asides into the Narrative

A common narrative technique allows narrators to relinquish their role for a few moments and utter asides intended to be heard by the audience, thus directing the listeners' attention away from the content and toward evaluation. As a result, the tellers not only align themselves with the victim in the story, but also pull the audience in to do the same. For example, "I was coming out of the subway station, and it was in the middle of the day, about 1:00 P.M. Oh, I guess it wasn't in the spring, because it was pretty cold out. I remember that" **(M-4)**. This confirmation of the fact during the telling is a way to emphasize that the event really did occur and to predispose the audience to accept the facts, however improbable they may be.

Tellers also make judgments about their own behavior as characters within the stories. For example, during the narration of a story, a teller might say, "So I was trapped" **(M-4)**. Comments about one's own behavior prior to the incident are common. "I was in a very good mood. That is always a liability in New York," said one mugging victim while describing how she was trapped in an elevator with an armed mugger **(M-23)**. Or, a teller may editorialize about the victim's actions, personality, or attributes. "He never thinks about geting hurt," one woman explained about a victimized friend **(M-15)**. Another technique is to judge others by making assumptions summarizing their actions, presented in asides in the narrative. For example, Irene Whitefield, when sharing Joe Bower's mugging in Greenwich Village (described earlier), said, "Joe didn't realize it, but the guy had a cane, a walking stick, and a knife." Joe, on the other hand, did not explain the event in the same way. While telling about a mugging victim, Ruth Melberg said, "Thank God they didn't hurt her. I don't know whether she lost money or not. . . . it's a frightening experience" **(M-34)**.

These three uses of asides in the story are ways to create a strong bond between the narrator and the listeners. While the teller and the audience may infuse the story with different meanings, it is the teller who can persuade the audience to attribute the same meaning to the stories through the use of asides. The teller can encourage sympathy for the victim, express an understanding of the precariousness of being the targeted victim, and guide the listener to the realization that the story about violence and its target is relevant for both teller and listener. Furthermore, the teller and the audience member may ask a common question: Who is a potential mugging victim? Editorializing in this manner is one way in which the teller can "weigh" the crime (i.e., "It wasn't serious") and try to come to an understanding of how violence is faced in everyday urban life.

Using Inference

Another narrative device that tellers use is inference. In this situation, the audience is provided with the barest of clues about the incident's outcome, and they then surmise the results. Inference is often used as a psychological safety valve. For some informants, relating the event may be emotionally difficult. Some incidents are almost too terrifying to put into words and are emotionally loaded. A parallel or obvious example, in our culture, is the euphemizing of death: one *buys the farm, kicks the bucket, passes on, or is laid to rest* rather than dies. In the same fashion, narrators of crime-victim stories often imply the conclusions rather than state them explicitly.

Inference functions in these stories by providing tellers with a common frame of reference. The narrators imply that a particular kind of crime situation has occurred, a rape or a mugging, for example, and the audience infers the results. In the following example, neither the teller nor the audience explains directly what has occurred. This narrative was collected from Ruth Melberg as she related it to a group of her neighbors:

> So, that's nothing! A woman comes into the lobby, and she's standing next to a colored man. He's standing next to her. She was a little hesitant. She says, "The elevator is slow." He says, "Yes, I've been waiting for about ten minutes." She says, "What floor are you going to?" So he says, "The fifth." She says, "Oh, I'm going to the fourth." So the elevator comes, and he goes into the elevator. She was afraid. So she waits until he goes up to the fifth floor and then comes down, right? So she goes in, goes up to the fourth floor, and he's waiting for her on the fourth floor! (M-36)

The implied message of the story is that one is never well enough prepared for these situations. The narrator warns about victimization in her own apartment complex, but never specifically delineates the event itself or its outcome. This stylistic strategy is a way in which both teller and audience use the narrative to meet on a common ground. The significance of these omissions and the use of inference indicate that the tellers and audience share a common frame of reference, a world view. The conclusion is not stated but is silently supplied by each party. Just as death is euphemized, so is victimization: it is expected to happen, but frightening to speak about.

Are these tales of city life true, or are they narcissistic accounts? Whether they are true or not does not diminish the fact that most people enjoy listening to a good story, especially one with which they can identify. On one level, these crime-victim narratives serve that function. The events discussed in them are often accepted as truth solely because they are so familiar, verifiable by degree. Who among a group of New Yorkers can deny hearing about a mugging or a murder? Simply put, these stories are believed to be true because they are so commonplace. The you-are-there effect, the empathy expressed for a person in danger, the human desire to see criminals "get their due," the insistence on warnings, and the rationalizations for gratuitous violence notwithstanding are elements that provide these narratives with unquestioned plausibility.

A frequent question that arises about the veracity of crime-victim stories is how they compare to written acounts of the same events. The purpose of comparing a written with an oral crime-victim narrative is to further elaborate how the oral story takes on its own distinctive stylizations, its own distinctive flavor. Throughout this chapter, the structural pattern of the orally reported crime-victim story, its stylization, its characterizations, and the embroidery techniques used in reporting it have been examined. In order to further establish the "traditional" oral character of the collected stories, comparisons between two oral and written accounts of the same incident will be discussed.[18]

Newspaper Accounts of Collected Crime-Victim Stories

Unlike the oral narrative, the newspaper account of a crime-victim incident is relatively more detailed and formulaic. First, the journalistic formula of the who, what, when, where, and how of the events is deftly incorporated into short paragraphs of long sentences filled with concrete details. Consequently, the written story lacks the suspense on which the oral account relies. The eye-catching headline provides the resolution to the story. Second, the newspaper account stresses the facts of the event, its place of occurrence, the roles played by the offender, the victim, the eyewitnesses, and especially the police. The reporter includes information about all these participants, identifying them by name, address, age, and often by occupation, but does not editorialize about their actions or speculate about them or the role each played in the incident. However, the major difference between the oral narrative and the newspaper account is the shift away from the event's impact on the victim towards a focus on the offender. For example, the newspaper story includes a short biographical sketch of the offender. It mentions any past criminal record and speculates on his or her motives. In general, the emphasis is on the suspect, not the victim.

Four collected narratives were corroborated with newspaper accounts. It is not surprising that so few stories were corroborated. Too many crime incidents go unreported to the police, let alone make it to the desk of a major metropolitan newspaper. And too many crime victims never tell their stories. Some events are told years later, and sometimes are confided to only a select few. Being victimized is never easy to confess. The two corroborated crime-victim stories discussed next concern sensationalized New York City murders. The written accounts attest the teller's presentation of the event, and they also show how these oral stories differ from their written counterparts.

The first narrative is entitled "Where's Ninth Avenue?" It was collected from Clara Gold and involves a murder in broad daylight near Herald Square in midtown Manhattan. A man came out of an Off Track Betting Office and asked directions from someone walking along the street. He then suddenly and unexpectedly shot the passerby. To Clara it seemed to be an unprovoked attack:

> In October of '73, there was a big stink in the newspapers at the time. On Thirty-fourth Street between Fifth and Sixth Avenue, you know, there's a Chock Full O'Nuts on the corner and a Chase Manhattan Bank further down the street. There's an OTB [Off Track Betting Office] right next to the Chock Full O'Nuts and the Chase Manhattan Bank. . . . a guy walked out of the OTB, stopped a passerby on the street, and said, "Excuse me, can you tell me how to get to Ninth Avenue?" And the guy, he turned around and said, "Oh, sure. What you do is just keep walking straight for two blocks." And the guy who asked the question said, "Thank you very much," and he [the questioner] pulled out a gun and shot him and a couple of passersby. The cops came. There were sirens all over the place. They had the whole street cordoned off, and they finally killed the guy in the subway, you know, the platform. Do you remember that? (**MR-1**)

Clara's rendition of the event clearly conforms to the common narrative structure previously outlined in these stories. The first portion of the story has its three recursive sequences. Clara introduces the time of the event (October of '73) first, and then the locale, providing evidence in the way of a familiar landmark to ensure that a common frame of reference is shared. Then she introduces the characters, two unknown urbanites. A confrontation is suggested, though a seemingly benign one, the common situation of asking for directions on a crowded Manhattan street. Next, dialogue is interjected: "Excuse me. Can you tell me how to get to Ninth Avenue?" Suddenly, the simple everyday scene is completely turned around. A man is shot in the street.[19] The story is resolved by the appearance of the police, and is completed with the coda. Clara asked her husband, Robert, who was present at the interview, if he too remembered the gruesome event. In sum, she personalized and localized the event, presented abstract characters, and stripped the story down to its basic component—

the shootout at midday. She related the second-hand account in the same manner in which first-person crime-victim narratives are told.

Unlike the oral narrative of the shootout on Thirty-fourth Street, the newspaper account describes fully the sequence of events that led up to the shooting and its aftermath; it also describes the people involved, including the 200 yelling bystanders.[20] While the news story lacks the suspense of the oral account—the headline anticipates the resolution—it contains flashbacks of the scenes of harrowing gunfight in broad daylight, eyewitness testimonials, full identification of the criminal involved and the request for directions, the subsequent confrontation with the passerby, the chase shootings down Thirty-fourth Street, and the resultant injuries and deaths. The newspaper report specifies the role that each person in the event played, unlike the oral account, where the characters are abstracted. In short, the newspaper account isolates the incident, singling it out as one episode from one day in the life of the city.

Just the opposite is true for the oral crime-victim account. Clara's account, and other narratives about crime victims, stress the folk attitude that these events are common, far from unusual. The oral story exhibits the folk attitude behind the story: frustration, fear of victimization, impotence on the part of urbanites. The oral story projects a shared perspective on the everyday: it represents the worst of urban living, implying that law and order is out of hand. The oral story stresses the personal. The newspaper story stresses the impersonal, the quelling of violence, the need for maintaining law and order, and the institutions of authority that do so.

The second corroborated story is entitled "The Security Guard" (**MR-13**). It was collected from Ruth Melberg, during the same interview session when the "The Apartment Sale" was recorded. The story is rather horrific: a young boy is thrown off a roof by a neighborhood security guard, and his body is discovered by his mother. Below is Ruth's tape-recorded version of the gruesome tale:

> Oh, I got a better one for you. Near the Coney Island Hospital there is an apartment complex. And they never had a security guard, but with all this going on the tenants got together and decided that they would hire a security guard. . . . and of course, he comes from an agency. Well, they did hire a security guard from Monday to Friday, since the man can't work seven days a week, so he worked five days a week. Then they got this part-time security guard to work on weekends. . . . [He] was recommended by the agency.
>
> Around the corner lived a little eight-year-old boy, and his mother comes out and says, "It's time to come in. It's seven o'clock." She says, "Come in, we are going to have dinner." He says, "I'll have one more ride, and then I'll come in." So the security guard, which is the part-time man, says to her, "Oh, don't worry about him. I'm the security guard around the corner. I'll

see to it that he doesn't cross the street with the bicycle." So she said, "Okay." So the security guard enticed this little boy with the bicycle up to the roof of this six-story apartment building. He molested him and then took the little boy and threw him off the roof. And so they called the mother. Naturally, when the mother saw her little boy laying on the floor dead, there was just no consoling her. When they investigated the security guard, they found out he had a record, that he was a molester. But it seems that the agency never sent his fingerprints to Albany and that when they asked for another security guard, they were in such a hurry to fill the position so that they can get their percentage, they just didn't bother sending his fingerprints to Albany. They recommended the next man that they had, and just unfortunately, it was this man who did have a police record. (**MR-13**)

In her version of the story, Ruth alleges that the security company's hasty decision, motivated by their greed, to hire the guard without checking his references, was directly responsible for the boy's death, which, she rationalizes, could have been prevented. She is also certain of several details that are disputed by the written account. In her story, the "weekend" guard was the murderer; yet, the day of the murder was on a Tuesday, not a Saturday or Sunday. Ruth also disclosed that the boy had been sexually abused, yet the medical examiner for the case found no such conclusive evidence. Clearly, the focus of Ruth's narrative emphasizes the horror of the event and its tragic consequences—the mother's discovery of her dead child. Compare this focus with the *New York Post* story:

A security guard was charged today with hurling a Brooklyn rabbi's 8 year-old son to his death from the roof of a six story apartment building in Sheepshead Bay.

Lawrence Gordon, 32, was employed as a guard in the Montauk Terrace Apartment complex where Nathan Scharf was slain, according to Detective Sgt. Gerrard Wilson.

Investigative sources said Gordon had been arrested previously for child molesting and that his wife had left him a few days ago.

Brooklyn Medical Examiner Milton Wald said he had come to no conclusion about whether the victim, found naked from the waist down, had been sexually molested. He said the boy died of fractures suffered in the plunge.

Gordon was not on duty when he encountered young Scharf in the neighborhood shortly before the boy's shattered body was found at the rear of 2885 E. Seventh Street, police said.

SERVED COMPLEX

The suspect who lives at 3054 Brighton Seventh St., Coney Island, was a part time employee of the Emergency Services Security Co., which has a contract to provide protection in the complex.

The boy's bicycle on the roof landing of 2685 E. Seventh St. led the police to believe he had been lured there and thrown to his death, possibly after resisting sexual overtures.

Fingerprints on the bicycle and an adult's footprint in the asphalt of the roof were two clues which helped lead to the arrest, investigators said.

Young Scharf, who lived at 731 Montauk Court, around the corner from where he had been killed, was the son of Rabbi and Mrs. Isak Scharf. He was last seen about 8 last night by his mother, Shirley.

The mother told police she had seen her son on his bicycle talking to a strange man on the street near their home. When the mother asked the man who he was he replied, "I'm all right, I'm one of the guards," police said.

A neighbor, Mrs. Jean Weissman recalled seeing Mrs. Scharf talking to her son. "She was asking him to come upstairs," Mrs. Weissman said. "He said he just wanted to ride his bike a few more times. . . ."[21]

Ruth underscored her telling of the story by insisting that the urban world is filled with untrustworthy people and unpredictable events.

In contrast to the typical newspaper accounts about crime, one significant feature of crime-victim narratives is the sanitizing of violence. One would predict that because of the overwhelming and constant portrayal of violence in the mass media, descriptions of violence would figure strongly in the stories. However, that is not the case. Informants commonly use euphemisms, such as he was "blown away," or he was "knocked off," or she was "ripped off," or he was "mugged." The last example is a slang term that could mean having one's pockets emptied or being shot to death. The reluctance to talk about violence in a concrete way, despite the fact that these accounts are defined as crime-victim stories by their tellers, creates an interesting paradox. Just as characters are abstracted, physical settings are undistinguished, and only particular details are emphasized, violence is quickly brushed over in the story. Though tellers and their audience are fascinated by the violence within the stories, they are also repelled by it. Identifying with the violence inflicted on the victim would mean confronting one's own vulnerability and, in turn, recognizing the gravity and possibility of being an urban target or survivor.

What conclusions can be drawn by looking at the style and structure of these tales about modern city life? Clearly, these stories are not snatches of urban folk conversations; they are structured and stylistically similar narratives about a common urban experience. For the folklorist, they provide an avenue for understanding how people shape daily experience into narratives, and, by extension, for inquiring further whether the ability to "create" stories with similar patterns, features, and structures is related to a universal human ability to fashion stories.[22] Why is it that when two different people get mugged at different times on different New York street corners, their stories are amazingly similar in style and structure? By identifying the traditional nature and features of stories, we can try to understand how stories are composed and how they are used by tellers, and how newly recognized traditions play an important role in our modern lives.

The personal-experience narrative is used as a vehicle to express an individual's or group's distillation of experience about important events and to present that experience in a meaningful way. Because of the pervasive (and invasive) role that crime and violence play in modern society, the crime-victim narrative is the most prevalent type of personal-experience story told today. These stories are about common situations: corroboration of the events by others or by written accounts is not essential to ensure their derivation as folk narrative. Everyone has his or her own story to tell, and because so many crime events occur daily, a corpus of traditional crime-victim stories comparable to other folk stories has yet to emerge. What is traditional, that is, expected and repeated, in these crime-victim stories are the common themes, character types, and, as shown in this chapter, internal features, structure, and stylistic details. It is these features that characterize these popularly told stories of urban life.

CHAPTER FOUR

The Functions of the Crime-Victim Narrative

City dwellers are bombarded by stimuli during the course of a day, and must adapt to an almost overwhelming environment. This is especially true in New York City, where a person could encounter over 11,000 people on his lunch hour. In public, New Yorkers and urbanites in general learn to be selective about where they walk, and to whom they speak and listen.[1] In so many situations, city dwellers must use their sharpened defense system, their antennae. This filtering system is part of an urban survival mechanism: it is an almost involuntary response to the overwhelming stimuli in the urban environment.[2] This refined system of self-protection can be jarred or interrupted as a result of crime victimization. One way to keep it functioning is to recognize and incorporate into daily behavior different ways to avoid being victimized. The crime-victim narrative serves that function: it tell of ways that urbanites can protect themselves.

Each day in New York City, hundreds of incidents occur that could be the seed for a personal-experience story. But not every experience becomes the basis for a story that is remembered and retold. For example, stories told to a small circle of intimates are often too esoteric to share.[3] Those that do have a larger audience often highlight unusual, extraordinary, incongruous, or humorous behavior. A narrative scholar, Livia Polyani, suggests that such shared stories can be reduced to terse cultural statements whose purpose is to send cultural messages from tellers to receivers.[4] For example, crime-victim narratives remind us how violent the culture and the city can be. They are culture-specific statements about New York City and urban life in general.

The crime-victim story has several other functions, as well. For example, like other forms of folk narrative, these particularly frightening accounts of urban violence serve as *cautionary tales*.[5] Their first purpose is to warn others about the dangerous streets of New York City. Their second purpose is didactic. They transmit a form of underground knowledge by imparting "street smarts." The narrators tell of specific methods that others can adopt in order to avoid becoming a crime victim. Third, the stories have therapeutic value. They enable victims and others concerned about crime to cope with traumatic experiences by allowing them to express their anger in a culturally sanctioned way. And, finally, these stories function as a source of entertainment: they tell of Woody Allen-like figures besieged by an unidentified paranoia, a fear of meeting up with an assailant and inevitable victimization.

But the main purpose of the crime-victim narrative as a cautionary tale is to warn listeners about the dangers of city living. The victim, already initiated into the evils of city life, is warning the uninitiated. Listeners not only are being warned about what happens to victims, they are also being advised about how to behave. "Hey, make sure you sit in the car with the conductor!" "I wouldn't walk through that park if I were you, pal." "You should watch out for that drunk on the next corner. He's really going nuts!" Explicit statements reinforce the advice implicit in the stories. Experience stands behind each piece of advice. As a result, each individual's account of a crime-victim's story symbolizes the possibilities of future dangerous encounters with crime. In other words, as is universally true with folk narrative, they provide guidelines for living.

One of the most common ways in which people speak about preventing crime victimization is by embedding safety tips into their stories. They provide advice on how not to become a victim—which is the second major function of these stories. Five of the most popular safety tips or crime-prevention skills are (1) have a good mental map of the city, (2) be inconspicuous, (3) learn some self-defense tactics, (4) avoid enclosed areas, and (5) cooperate with your assailant.

Lesson 1: Have a Good Mental Map of New York City

I spoke with many people who claimed that having a complete mental map of New York provided them with some protection against crime. But while many insisted on this tip, their knowledge of New York City was inconsistent. They claimed to know several Manhattan neighborhoods or outlying boroughs rather well; but commonly they lacked knowledge of neighborhoods other than their own and one or two more. And some people expressed a reluctance to visit new areas: "I've lived in Brooklyn all my life," said one twenty-eight-year-old woman, "and, you know, I don't think I've ever been to the Bronx. Why go?" Midtown Manhattan, where many informants worked, was the exception. Most people knew the major areas and districts: the Garment Center, the Theater District, Wall Street, for example. That few informants had a good working knowledge of

New York, even though they claimed that this was needed, was not surprising. Kevin Lynch, for example, discovered a similar pattern, while interviewing Bostonians. He realized that many Bostonians could find significant historical landmarks in downtown Boston, but like some of the people I spoke with, they were ignorant about surrounding neighborhoods.[6]

Knowledge of New York City also seemed to run across ethnic, occupational, and even racial lines. Most whites I spoke to knew little of Harlem, called it off limits, or used it, as in the example below, as a way to indicate a lack of knowledge:

> I can remember one time—this is an incident that happened to me. . . . a violent thing. It was one summer, and I was going with this girl, and this was about '65. I said, "Why don't we take a bike drive to Harlem?" . . . we left about six o'clock at night. We rode down there, and I said, "It's safe, don't worry." She said, "Well, you sure it's safe?" I said, "Don't worry." So we rode down there, and we were on . . . where was it? I'd say in the 130s, and we're riding . . . she was in back of me . . . and I was in front. And a bottle misses us by about five feet. It splatters, and we hear someone saying, "Get out of here, whitey." Something like that. So . . . we cut short our tour and headed up this wide street, you know, and out of Harlem as quickly as we could! . . . now, I wouldn't even walk there. I would walk on the wide street side of Harlem but not the side streets. I'd be afraid. I wouldn't be as afraid of 125th Street as I would be of Lenox Avenue [major crossroads]. (M-29)

In the above example, the informant, Robert Ross, uses the story as an example of what he considers to be his own ignorance. But he also does something else, which is common. He alters his subsequent behavior to avoid the side streets of Harlem.

"Cognitive mapping," often discussed by environmental psychologists and urban sociologists, includes knowing an area well and having a map of the area in one's head.[7] Cognitive maps allow people to find their way and provide individuals with a sense of security and safety. They remind people that their environment can be trusted and depended on:

> When I come home from work, late at night, even if I'm lucky enough to park my car right in front of my apartment building, I have my keys in my hand. I know the streets well. I know every house on the street, but I still have those keys in my hand.[8]

Sociologists Robert LeJeune and Nicolas Alex, when interviewing mugging victims, discovered that victims felt safer once on home territory. Victims were often surprised that they were vulnerable to crime in areas that they used daily and presumed safe.[9] Many of the stories I collected here had that same familiar ring. "Can you imagine, being mugged in your own elevator?" said an elderly woman who had lived in the same apartment building for over forty years without incident.

Nevertheless, people I spoke with claimed that having a good cognitive map of an area was a deterrent to victimization. As a result of hearing about a crime incident, or being victimized themselves, many people indicated that they had significantly altered their cognitive maps and took additional precautions to afford themselves an added sense of security. For example, it is not uncommon for a woman to move to a new apartment or new neighborhood after a rape.[10] And some women seemed more wary of particular subway stations where several rapes had occurred. In order to feel more secure, some, like Irene Whitefield, a secretary and part-time actress, made up their own "superstitions" or guideposts and personalized their individual cognitive maps:

> I've been walking home lately. We've been having our rehearsals in the Pan Am building. I would get out about ten, ten-thirty, and I would be walking home alone. And that really got to me. I walked straight down Fifth Avenue and over to Sixteenth Street. I was a little tense because it was so deserted down here. It's funny, because you make up your own superstitions. My halfway street is Twenty-ninth Street. There's a reader's advisor on that block that's open to about one o'clock. It's the *only* thing that is open for about fifteen to twenty blocks. Once you get past Thirty-fourth street. . . . So I thought, Gee, if anything happens, I could run to the reader's advisor and say, "Forget about telling my fortune! Call the police!![11]

In the crime-victim stories themselves, mental mapping is a prominent feature. Informants are quick to include the time and place of a victimization, thus enhancing the mental map of the listeners and sharpening their conceptual view of the city. It also allows them to judge which areas the narrators assume are safe and which are dangerous. The narrators use the story as a didactic tool to exert their influence on their audience. They try to persuade the listeners—the potential victims—to avoid what the tellers perceive as threatening territory. That is, they are asking others to change their perceptual maps of New York City, based on the narrator's personal experiences or those of others. Whether that advice is heeded, and over what period of time, is difficult to discern.

Lesson 2: Be Inconspicuous

During the course of my interviewing, people constantly reiterated the importance of street smarts: of being aware of one's surroundings, and being able to react to potentially dangerous situations. Some informants, particularly women, devised their own folk methods of self-protection. Kate Whitefield said:

> I decided my main rule of thumb is that if I'm walking down a street I'm not familiar with and if it's totally deserted, and somebody is making a point to come near me, then it doesn't look too good. If anybody gets close enough, say within arm's reach, friend or foe, they're going to get bopped with my bag. Then I'm taking off.[12]

Other women had different tactics, such as carrying scissors, cans of mace, or umbrellas. Like Kate, several women assumed that they could use their pocketbooks as weapons; in fact, one woman, after being assaulted on the street, carried a can of condensed soup in her purse for over a year![13] If informants thought they were in danger, for example, if they were being followed, they relied on more practical tactics than soup cans. They might crisscross the street several times, or walk past their homes, duck into a store or restaurant, and call for help. Many women I spoke to also avoided late-night subway rides in favor of expensive taxis, or avoided the subway altogether. Others rely on their own intuition, their "sixth sense," if they suspect danger:

> My friend Arthur calls me up. . . . He says, "Mary, there's a guy running around your neighborhood." He started describing him. He says, "Be careful. Don't go to the laundry room unless there's people there. I know it's easy to go there alone, but make sure that there's somebody there with you." So I go to tell this to another girl who lives in my building, and I started describing him. She said, "Sure, chubby, black hair, beard." I was looking at her, and I said, "I didn't say all this yet." She says, "I know who you are talking about. He was in our laundry room." I said, "Ellen, are you okay?" She said, "Mary, you know how you get vibrations from people. . . . He walked into our laundry room . . . and I was folding up laundry, and I *just got bad vibrations* from this guy. And I just walked out. I went upstairs to get my husband. I told my husband what happened, and he started laughing, thinking I was paranoid. The whole bit. She said, "Well, your laundry is downstairs. I'm not going down there unless you come with me." **(R-7)**

Included in these lessons about avoiding urban crime was one consistent warning: be inconspicuous and you can avoid being a target. For example, one suggestion was to dress inconspicuously in public, referred to by one narrator as "melting in with the crowd." In the city environment, especially in New York City where fashion is so esteemed, dress is certainly a distinctive marker. Some people that I spoke to had elaborate explanations for using their appearance as a weapon against victimization. One young man wanted to "appear tough" and told me he wore leather jackets Brando-style.[14] But more common was an explanation such as Ellen Schwartz's:

I walk home from the subway early in the morning. The other morning I
came home at two o'clock in the morning. I was the *only* woman and the
only white on the entire Seventh Avenue IRT subway. And the object is to
look as *tough* as you can and to put it on in an odd way. . . . I try to avoid
wearing skirts on the subway, even though I like wearing skirts and looking
feminine and pretty. You *have* to *look ugly.* You've got to look *mean,* and
you've got to *look poor.* And you've got to *look inconspicuous.* Like Tess of
the D'Urbervilles—wrapping her face up in bandages so she won't have to
get disturbed on the moors. That's the way you have to travel late at night in
New York. Otherwise, you're a prisoner in your own house.[15]

Lyn Lofland, in *A World of Strangers,* comments on the role that
appearance has played in both the preindustrial city and the modern urban
center. According to Lofland, in preindustrial cities, where public space
had multiple uses and where city activities were spatially integrated, an
individual's appearance was crucial. People were "type-cast" by their
clothes; identified according to a particular class or occupation. However,
the people in the modern city are not as easy to distinguish.[16] The modern
city, especially New York City, is known for its heterogeneity. And since
outward appearance is not always a distinguishing characteristic of identification, it is difficult to tell the offenders from the victims.

People think I'm crazy or I'm paranoid. On the other hand, they are not
doing what I am doing. I'm not a prisoner in my own house. I go anywhere I
damn please, BUT with precaution. So when the weather is cool enough,
I'll usually wear flat shoes, good for running and kicking. If it is really
winter, I'll wear a down jacket that makes my shoulders look really big.
Then you can't tell how petite and slight I really am. You stand there, you
see, and you can stand with your arms pronated. It makes your shoulders
look bigger. That's a masculine stance . . . to turn your arms out. . . .
You're standing there with your arms pronated, and your feet are sort of
planted. And don't look anybody in the eye. . . . don't make eye contact
with anybody. . . . This is the 2:00 A.M. routine.[17]

The folk belief that dress and appearance are tied to victimization was
reinforced while I was conducting fieldwork in 1981. During that time, the
wearing of gold chains became popular. Wearing flashy jewelry defies the
"rule" of appearing inconspicuous and makes the fashionable New Yorker
an easy target for a street mugger. The New York City subway becomes
the contemporary counterpart of the Hollywood western and its stage
coach robbery scene:

The only other story I knew that I was witness to was in the subway. I was
riding the subway—the RR local—home, and the train itself was different.
Most of the subway windows are tilted when you open them. This subway
train had happened to have windows which came down like regular win-

dows. And it wasn't crowded, but every seat was taken. And these two young boys came in. It was summer. It was hot. They weren't wearing shirts. They were wearing cut-off jeans. Cut off at the thigh. They came in, walked up and down in the car. I guess they must have been looking at the people. They went to the doorway. And then the train stopped, and they got out. From where I was sitting, I saw them standing there, and I thought it was very odd. After all, if they did get out, why aren't they walking out the exit. But just before the train started, one of them LEAPED into the air, cata-pulting himself about halfway in through an open window. And all I could think of at the time was that he was going to fall over the girl. If he made a mistake, why didn't he go back into the train? What kind of way is that to enter a train, sliding through a window? But actually, what he did was grab the chain, so that he must have been canvassing when they were walking up and down the train to see who was a likely victim. And she was sitting under this open window. But she had this long hair, and it got tangled up in her hair. And with the first pull . . . she reached up and grabbed it. . . . His timing was perfect, because he jumped up in the train just before the train moved on, and he had only a moment to grab it. And she fooled him, because she had to jump back, or he would have been carried away by the moving train. Of course she was hysterical, and of course her neck was burned. . . . She was with her friend or her husband, who tried to console her. And he looked at her and said, "What do you want me to do?" (M-77)

A friend of mine realized that he was getting set up on the subway. He has a very flashy watch. . . . He saw these two dudes sitting across from him. One of them pointed at his own wrist. My friend realized that he was probably going to get hit when he left the subway. So he got out at the next subway stop, and he walked very close to the subway. They did stand up and follow him. And just as the doors were about to close, he jumped in and took off and continued his ride. I think he said the guys were left standing there outside and cursing. (M-51)

The narratives above underscore the didactic role that these stories play. Each warns about the suddenness of being a victim. As a result of these common victimizations, many people I spoke with, particularly women, no longer wear jewelry; of if they do, they conceal it. One woman com-mented, "What a shame. I used to wear jewelry for sentimental reasons; now I'm too frightened to do even that."

Lesson 3: Learn Some Self-Defense Tactics

Informants spoke of other ways they thought they could defend them-selves against crime, especially in public. Suggestions included wearing money belts, carrying no money at all, carrying only credit cards, or doing without a pocketbook. One woman pinned dollar bills to her clothes; one man stuck some bills in his sock. Others cited avoidance as their self-defense tactic. For example, some avoided subway lines, office buildings, or certain public places, such as Central Park. Most of the people I spoke with were constantly on the alert for any unexpected danger. This is one tenet of being street smart, as the following example suggests:

> The other day I was walking in Brooklyn. I went to my girlfriend's house. And I was walking down the block. And my girlfriend was living in a neighborhood like this. And this man opens his blade and he starts laughing at me. And I looked at him. I was a little scared because I had a little child with me. So I picked up the child, and I started walking fast. But you know, I realized that if you argue to try to get brave, it's gonna lead to trouble. If you could avoid things, why not? **(M-67)**

Maria Diaz, who gave me the advice above, included a clear message: Learn how to protect yourself by minimizing interaction in a tense situation. Many tellers of other narratives imparted this urban folk knowledge. For Susan Roberts, a single woman traveling from Manhattan to Brooklyn, being street smart is important:

> Well, last night I was at a friend's house in the city on the West Side. There was a whole group of people there, and we were all playing Scrabble. I really had to get home at eleven o'clock. Everyone had to stop what they were doing, walk me to the train because she [the hostess] was too afraid to walk me to the train and come back by herself. It was now like a group activity. They walked me to the train and waited until the train came. . . . Instead of getting off at a local stop and walking to my apartment [in Brooklyn], I got off at the express [stop], where I knew I could get a taxicab. Then, I am going out of my way for safety. I mean, everything is extra time and extra money. I had to take a taxi home.[18]

Susan Roberts mentioned what many other informants emphasized: street smarts take extra time, and sometimes extra money. Being street smart means planning ahead. An important way that these urban crime stories are put to use is by providing listeners with concrete guidelines for the future: they tell listeners how to protect themselves.

Lesson 4: Avoiding Enclosed Areas

Many informants spoke of isolated and enclosed areas such as subway cars, apartment- and office-building elevators, stairwells, vestibules, and public restrooms as generally unsafe areas. The lesson in their stories is obvious: avoid entrapment if you want to avoid being victimized. Some informants, including Bernadette Potter and Daniel Miller, whose narratives appear below, seemed particularly frustrated by this axiom, since the subway was their only means of transportation, and such common advice was problematic. Almost all the people I spoke to told of events happening on the subway: teenagers harassing older people, unsavory panhandlers, holdups. During an interview, Bernadette commented:

> There are some [subway] stops that are very long. They go from point A to point B, and they'll take three, four, maybe five minutes to get there because they have to go under tunnels . . . especially when you are going from borough to borough. Those stops tend to be long. And there have been a lot of robberies inside subway cars. . . . You're almost trapped, when you think about it. If you think about it in that way, you're trapped in that one car. And there are people who started to rob people, especially in those trains.[19]

The following narrative certainly underscores her point. The story involves a man attending a professional conference in New York City. He and his friend, a tourist, decided to take a trip on the Staten Island ferry. Their short subway ride turned into one of the most frightening experiences of his life:

> I met a woman there [at the convention], and we just had to get away from the round of interviews. . . . We decided to go to Staten Island and take the ferry to get away. It was after work hours but not terribly late, six o'clock. We took the subway to South Ferry, and we were all dressed up. We must have looked like a wealthy couple. We were all dressed up for our interviews. The subway makes a circle around New York's periphery. It's sharply banked. All of the stations are on one side; all the doors are open on one side for five or six stations running. Being in New York, where I have all my survival skills, I always sit on one of the cars next to the conductor, knowing that the conductor has to walk back and forth to open the doors. So we sat in one of these places.
>
> Two guys came in, and they already figured out that the conductor wouldn't be in for the next six stations—came in, and they took a look at us. Immediately, I knew what we were in for. They came back with their guns. They were both obviously stoned, high on something or other. One of them was trying to be very comical. "Excuse me, but we are going to rob you. We would like all your money, please. Please take off your wristwatches, please." The other guy had a gun to my head. He was obviously more jumpy: "Come on, or we'll blow your fucking head off!" That was the refrain. "Now, will you kindly take off your jacket so I can search the inside pocket," and "We'll blow your fucking heads off!" They found that neither of us had wristwatches. They opened my wallet, found a bunch of credit cards, looked at them. Between us we had $4.17. I said, "Excuse me, we are going to a job interview. We only look fancy, but we are really both poor." And the other guy said, "Good, so we'll blow your fucking head off! Are you sure you ain't holding out on me?" He took off my coat, ripped off the side pockets, ripped out all the lining to make sure that I didn't have a secret money belt. Took off my belt and simply walked off with my belt when he found it wasn't a money belt. And again, the guy said, "We are

going to leave the train now. Sit, keep seated, don't call out until you have reached one more station." So the two of them disappeared. (M-55)

In addition to subway cars, elevators were trigger zones that informants considered dangerous. One victim who was attacked with a knife in an elevator said that she knew she "had made a big mistake" when she got into the elevator with her attacker. Others are less suspecting:

A friend of mine bought a newspaper one evening. And as he was walking home—as he was just ready to come into the house—there were a few boys waiting in the lobby which he didn't see. But once they got into the elevator, then they pounced on him. They beat him up very badly. They didn't want anything, they just wanted to beat him up. (M-11)

In the following example, Ellen Axelrod was caught off guard, like most victims, while standing in her apartment-building vestibule. After all, an apartment vestibule may seem like "safe" territory because of its familiarity:

It was a Sunday evening about six-thirty . . . in January about three or four years ago in the house I'm living in now. I came in the house, and I was very tired. I had been at a meeting all day long. So, I was carrying my pocketbook, and I had some pockets with lots of papers and stuff, and I didn't get my key out ahead of time. And I got into the vestibule part, you know, before the door with the lock. And I was dragging myself along. I wasn't paying attention to such stuff, and my pocketbook and all that I was carrying just dumped out all over the stairs. And I said, "Oh shit!" And I moved over slowly. And it was in the winter, so there weren't a lot of people around me, and I wasn't swift. . . . I took my time. I was looking at my papers, and I looked at my key. But I was just about collected when I heard somebody rush in through the door. And he had his hand in his pockets like this as if he had a gun [gestures]. . . . "I don't want to hurt you. Just give me the money." And again, I was calm while it was happening. But then I was furious, so I ran out the door chasing him. I was mad because I had papers in there. He had gotten everything, the checkbook. I didn't have any charge cards at the time—but I had a driver's license, registration, and all that, plus it was the first time I had bought a real leather pocketbook. I had spent fifty bucks. It was a week old. I was so pissed. If he had just taken the cash . . . I think I had about sixty bucks in there. But he got everything. So I was just so pissed. Anyway, I went upstairs and called the police. Not because I thought they would catch him, but because it had all my identification in there, and I wanted to get it all on record. . . . Nothing was ever found. But, I didn't lose anything more than sixty bucks, because he never cashed any checks. (M-85)

Lesson 5: Cooperate with Your Assailant

Ellen commented about how she was in the vestibule area, an enclosed place, right before the assailant rushed in. She also included another common safety tactic about how not to become a physically injured victim: cooperate with the assailant. Ellen and others consistently spoke of how foolish it is to antagonize an assailant. Since street mugging, for example, is often an impetuous act on the part of the offender, and targets are often chosen at random, victims have no advance warning.[20] Most informants I interviewed claimed that they were unsuspecting and caught in a random circumstance. Maria recalled the following incident thirteen years after its occurrence:

> I was in the elevator with a friend of mine. I was very young. I was about ten years old at the time I was being mugged. My teenage years were spent in Puerto Rico. When I was in New York, in elementary school, I used to go to my aunt's place and take the elevator. We were very calm and relaxed. We were talking. We bought some cake, and I had a bag [pocketbook]. It was Sunday. I was dressed up, and my friend was dressed up nice. And this guy comes into the elevator and puts a blade on us. But my friend didn't see it, and I caught it first. "Look! Look!" My girlfriend wasn't aware of what was happening, and then she saw the blade, and she started to scream hysterically. I mean SCREAMING HYSTERICALLY. Then I wanted to find out what he wanted. I see the blade, and he keeps going like this [motions with hand], and he's getting nervous and she's screaming so much. He's getting nervous. See, he might go crazy and start cutting me up! She's screaming, and I'm nervous. My legs feel shaky. But I'm trying to find out what he wants so he could leave me alone. So I tell her to be quiet. He keeps going like this [motions], so, maybe, he wants my bag, and he takes it. So then he's still going like this [motion with hand]. He wants something. He keeps going like this with his blade. I wonder what he wants. The cake was on the floor, so I gave it to him. So then he's supposed to beat it, right? So I said, "Here, take this. Here's some cake." I wanted to give him anything. I just wanted him to leave us alone. My girlfriend was urinating on herself. She did it on herself. She ruined her stockings. She was really scared. It was funny, you know, because I handed the guy the cake, and he said, "No, I'm not hungry." And he left. He went with two pocketbooks. I didn't have much money. I had about three dollars. But my girlfriend felt bad because she had about forty dollars in her pocketbook. She had a new leather bag. But I'm not the type to carry money, because I know so many things happen in New York. When I go shopping, I don't even carry money. I carry credit cards. I have credit cards now in every store. . . . But you NEVER think about it until it actually happens. **(M-48)**

The story above tells how some people react to danger and how helpless they feel when caught in a dangerous situation. Certainly, those in jeopardy must quickly assess the situation: whether rape victims should fight off their attackers or acquiesce to their demands is an unresolved question. Many victims editorialize about their actions: "I was so angry, I ran after her, which was a stupid thing to do!" said one elderly lady after being viciously attacked by a young woman in her building elevator. Anger was a common response to victimization, but according to the people I interviewed, revenge was not. In the example below, the teller speaks of the helplessness that many victims feel after being personally threatened, especially if they do cooperate. In this instance, there seemed little that the victim could do but accept her fate:

> Oh, I'll give you a better one than that. Two friends of mine are coming home in a cab from a business dinner, my friend and his sister. They are in a taxicab. It's in the middle of the summer. The windows are open. The cab driver stops for a red light. Now they are passengers. They're inside there riding. My friend had her pocketbook on her lap. [They] stopped at a crosswalk for a red light. All of a sudden, through the open window an arm comes through the open window, shoves her sister, grabs the pocketbook, and runs. This is through an open window! What do you do? Absolutely nothing. . . . Her sister [the teller's friend] was horrified because her sister and the cab driver got out of the cab and chased the guy. She was sitting there quivering, and her sister—the idiot—is running out there to chase the guy! (**M-72**)

Crime victims do suffer to varying degrees from violation and stress reactions. Crime victims I spoke to experienced these reactions less frequently and less severely in attacks on property than in acts of bodily harm, such as rape. Minimizing the resulting personal agony, fear, and anxiety is difficult. In these situations, victims are suddenly frightened and are caught totally off guard. Their adrenalin starts to pump, their hands may shake, their thinking may be foggy and confused, all a result of being caught unaware and defenseless. Adults usually pride themselves on controlling their actions, but a sudden confrontation with an offender momentarily changes their status and quickly robs them of their personal autonomy. Quite suddenly, they are under the control of another person, often an armed and powerful one. Cooperation is essential. In other words, as crime-victim specialists Morton Bard and Dawn Sangrey write: "Crimes that involve personal confrontation threaten autonomy much more directly. In any face-to-face encounter with a criminal the victim is painfully aware that his or her survival is on the line. Whether the threat is stated or implied, the loss of autonomy is absolute—the victim surrenders control on pain of death."[21]

The above-mentioned safety tips—have a good cognitive map, look inconspicuous, use some self-defense techniques, avoid enclosed areas, and avoid antagonizing an assailant—are all ways to attempt to maintain control over one's territory. They provide urbanites with some sense of security. Not only do the tips and the stories themselves provide insight into how people react to victimization, they also indicate ways for people to take their safety into their own hands.

Personal-experience narratives, such as the ones about crime discussed here, provide a way for individuals to be in the limelight. After all, the experience itself may be common but not for the victim. Telling a traumatic or exciting story of encountering danger or death can be a way to garner praise, attention, or short-lived notoriety. The teller's status is elevated, especially when the victim/teller speaks of how heroically he or she acted during the time of danger, which may not actually be the case.[22] In my experience, it seemed that victims were often able to acknowledge their lack of power and their submissiveness during the incident. One of the reasons for telling these personal-experience stories is so that victims can appear victorious over situations they could not control. Individuals seeking to gain power over the experience through words are simply retelling a structured narrative. Relating their role in the story is a way for them to bring the danger under control and reclaim their self-esteem.

Recounting the incident rather than repressing it can be helpful in dealing with its aftermath. Thus, storytelling itself is a mark of survival. For example, rape crisis centers establish an environment in which victims can speak without fear, recrimination, or blame and in an atmosphere of support. By telling their stories, by ordering the events and placing them in perspective, rape victims and others affected by crime can resolve the trauma of their experiences. Telling the story becomes therapeutic.

The victim often goes through several stages in overcoming a crime victimization, similar to the stages of accepting death outlined by Elisabeth Kübler-Ross: denial, anger, acceptance, and resolution.[23] While collecting these stories, I interviewed people who were in various stages as a result of victimization. For example, some were at the point of denying the experience and questioning its validity. It was not uncommon to hear, "I couldn't believe this was happening to me!" Others, though only a handful, harbored feelings of hostility and revenge toward the criminals, which for some continued over a period of years. One rape victim said, "I'll kill him if I ever see him again!"

Because crime-victim experiences are so rampant, and because these narratives are so often heard—as testimonials, as eyewitness accounts, as shared personal-experience stories—their retelling has power. Such stories are the common fare of several occupational groups—policemen, lawyers, medical and mental-health professionals, newscasters, and ministers, to name a few. Our culture values "getting it off your chest" and the idea that sharing the experience can afford relief to the victims and those affected by crime. The widespread popularity and growth of support groups for victims of all types and experiences would attest to this notion. Crime-victim stories not only are told because they function as a coping mechanism to deal with traumatic events (as with other types of personal-experience narratives); they also provide a way in which victims can garner support and empathy from listeners, and reduce their feelings of isolation. Listeners may offer supportive responses such as, "Yeah, I know what you mean," or "Yes, I know what you're going through."[24] Such support is one reason that stories are often told in a competitive way, each person trying to top another's experience. The message to the victim is that others have gone through similar incidents that are also disturbing and horrendous. They allow tellers to cope and to deal with these events by providing vehicles for them to express their rage and hostility toward offenders, and even give voice to their fantasies of revenge in a culturally acceptable way. As mentioned in the Introduction, narrators of crime-victim stories could be both sullen and depressed when sharing their experiences. However, there were several times when they exploded into robust laughter, laughing at themselves, the antics of the offender, or the nature of the situation. In relation to crime victims, laughter and jocular word play have three main uses: (1) to express anxiety about reestablishing one's sense of the world as a safe and dependable place to live, (2) to help the victim regain his or her sense of autonomy, and (3) to distance oneself from the emotional pain of the violation that the experience has incurred. All three purposes help victims cope with the trauma of the event.

Clearly, the crime-victim stories not only fulfill the three functions mentioned above, but they also display a particular type of urban humor, like that found in the social comedy of performers such as Rodney Dangerfield, Robert Klein, David Steinbrenner, and particularly Woody Allen. Allen, a raconteur of the foibles of urban life, often uses New York City as the backdrop for his films. In most of these films, he reveals himself to be an anxious urban misfit, victimized by people, by crime, and by love relationships. Audiences identify with the Allen character; they recognize those aspects of contemporary life he so poignantly ridicules. Allen's humor recognizes that anxiety is the most significant and shared feature of urban life, and it constantly exposes his fears (and ours) about crime and violence, parental authority, ethnic intolerance, hypochondria, success, sex, and relationships. Allen reminds us about our own self-doubts, fears, and weaknesses, and our ability to deal with modern life in a major metropolis.[25] His jokes about using several locks to bolt his apartment shut, or his squeamishness about and fear of being attacked at night in the streets are common urban folk attitudes. He projects these shared urban fears in his films in the same way New Yorkers do when they tell crime-victim stories. By laughing with Allen, and by laughing with narrators, we recognize our own human weaknesses. By laughing at the situation, we attempt to distance and control it. And instead of letting crime overwhelm us, we recognize that others have experienced and suffered, as well. As a result, we can attempt to reestablish the world as we knew it before the victimization—acceptably safe, dependable, trustworthy.

The people I spoke with were amused by stories in which the criminal appeared stupid or foolish. The story that first comes to mind is one mentioned previously, about the rapist who accepted from the victim a personal check made out to his name. Stories that were told in a jocular way pale once in print. But they do seem to provide tellers with some sense of superiority. These tales, like numskull stories, highlight the stupidity of the criminal who is able to start a crime but not smart enough to execute it successfully. In this form of humor, victims and tellers seem to triumph over the weakness and stupidity of their offenders.

Humor comes in many varieties (political, ethnic, black, gallows), addresses several human situations, and is used differently in different groups, structures, and types. But regardless of its use, humor works only when it is an expression of the collective experience of the participants and receives response only from those who have common concerns. The common concerns here include victimization, assault, and paranoia, which present a kind of urban humor. Humor here works as a safety valve to express the fears and anxieties about living in such a frenetic environment as New York City. By laughing at the criminals, tellers and their audience can say, "Look at that fool! He's trying to break the law, and he's too stupid to figure out how to do it!" By laughing at the offender, the victim is no longer psychologically submitting to his or her control or authority. And by laughing, victims can emotionally distance themselves from the victim experiences in general. A reversal of roles can occur, one of the bases of all comedy. The criminal becomes the weakling; the victim becomes triumphant. In other words, by finding some comedy in the situation, tellers are able to objectify the experience and reduce some of the emotional trauma that often accompanies victimization, allowing them to cope with the event itself.[26] Finding humor in these stories about violence, pain, and suffering was not all that surprising. Laughter itself, as Norman Cousins has discussed, has therapeutic value, allowing people to reconnect with others and reminding them of a shared sense of what makes people human.[27]

Generally speaking, one of the main reasons that victims share these stories about urban life is the desire to tell and warn others how *not* to become a crime victim. Many times their advice, as we have here, is direct; that is, they use the narrative itself as a warning device. Sometimes, their clues about protection are more subtle and are embedded within the story and deduced by the listeners. But whether implicitly or explicitly, tellers impart a form of folk knowledge—street smarts. In addition, these stories teach about the dangers of the urban world. They function as a psychological safety valve, permitting tellers and victims to objectify their experiences by finding some humor in them. And by telling their stories, victims can start to regain their sense of autonomy, so often robbed from them during victimization.

CHAPTER FIVE

World View and the Crime-Victim Narrative

New York City occupies a unique place in America's popular culture, as well as in its folklore.[1] It is constantly depicted as a dangerous, crime-filled metropolis in both movies and popular television detective programs. In *Death Wish,* a Hollywood film that has received considerable audience attention, Charles Bronson portrays a man who decides to avenge single-handedly the deaths of his wife and daughter, who were viciously attacked in their Manhattan apartment by a group of delinquents. Bronson's character stalks Central Park and Manhattan streets after dark, brazenly attacking street thugs before (he assumes) they attack him or other New Yorkers. His vendetta against urban crime brings cheers of support from movie audiences.[2] This film and its two sequels, *Death Wish II* and *Death Wish III,* can be added to a score of others that use New York as their backdrop to emphasize urban crime. Television police detective shows, which also have a wide national audience, frequently use New York City as their setting. Programs such as "Kojak," "Barney Miller," "Cagney and Lacey," and "The Equalizer" provide American viewers with a weekly dose of the city's darker side.

This popular-culture depiction of crime, violence, and victimization as integral to daily life in New York City is reinforced in several examples of folklore that have had a broad national currency. Folklorist Jan Harold Brunvand, for example, reports several versions of an urban legend about baseball player Reggie Jackson, who meets up with two elderly women tourists in a New York City elevator. Jackson is in the elevator with his pet dog and shouts at the animal to sit. Immediately, the women sit down on the elevator floor. Jackson apologizes to the women, explaining that he was speaking to his pet. Once the nervous women recover, they ask Jackson for suggestions about dining out, and decide to go to the restaurant he recommends. When they try to pay their bill, they discover that the man in the elevator, who they come to learn is the famous baseball star, has paid it.[3] While the legend reaffirms Jackson's superstar status, it also hints at the tourists' fear of crime and society's racist attitudes. An important, but neglected, aspect of the discussion of this legend is its setting: New York City is invariably used as the backdrop.[4] Because New York City is consistently perceived as a crime capital, the locale is rarely scrutinized. Nevertheless, its mere mention lends believability to the depicted event. Would the legend have the same effect if the alleged incident happened in Cleveland or Altuna?

Some folkloric examples about New York City or depictions of New Yorkers involve humor. For example, during the popular lightbulb joke cycle several years ago, one joke was particularly striking in its presentation of New Yorkers. In this joke, one New Yorker asks another, "How many New Yorkers does it take to change a lightbulb?" The reply? "What's it to ya?" This response presents the New Yorker as someone unwilling to divulge even the simplest information, to the point of being cautiously rude and hostile. This joke, however, was also told by informants, New Yorkers among them. Some acknowledged with a bit of pride that New Yorkers had a recognizable persona, however unlikeable. By transmitting the joke, they too acknowledged the stereotype of New Yorkers as rude and uncivil. On the other hand, New York City humor projected by New Yorkers reveals a certain tenacity and strength based on what one commentator calls "a survival instinct," which he claims is unexhibited elsewhere and is probably misunderstood by those not living in New York City.[5] As mentioned earlier, the joke about carrying extra money for muggers, or the quips told at the tea previously described serve as examples of this cynical, tenacious humor.

It was the Bernhard Goetz incident that reinforced the image of New York City as a crime capital. On December 22, 1984, Goetz, a bespectacled, owlish-looking white male who worked as an electronics engineer, took a subway ride that significantly changed his life. Dubbed "Death Wish Killer" or the "Subway Vigilante" by the city's sensationalistic media, Goetz became a controversial, though short-lived, urban folk hero. On the subway that night, he had whipped out a revolver from his waistband and shot four black teenagers who approached him with sharpened screwdrivers and demanded five dollars for video games, "I've got five dollars for each one of you," replied Goetz as he aimed his revolver at the youths.

To many New Yorkers, Goetz became a cause célèbre. Stories about him headlined newspapers everywhere. Even T-shirts bearing his likeness were sold on Manhattan street corners. Goetz—as the victim who struck back—acted atypically when compared to the characters described in these crime-victim stories. Goetz projected the fears and frustrations of all crime victims and potential victims, and reinforced a well-known image of New York City. Furthermore, the event solidified New York as the symbol of the most violent and dangerous American city in the world's imagination.[6]

Certainly, the international attention garnered by Goetz and the sensationalism by the media made the incident as powerful as the 1964 Genovese murder. But in the Goetz case, the interest in this urban figure reached its peak when he was an anonymous, mysterious fugitive from the law turning himself in at a police station in New Hampshire. As the facts of the case were revealed to the public and Goetz's personality and past experiences were scrutinized, he began to lose his supporters.[7] As in the common crime-victim experiences cited in these stories, the Goetz incident is another example onto which the fears of the city's people were projected: only his case was more dramatic. Another difference between the Goetz case and the crime-victim stories discussed here is the refusal to submit to an offender's power. Goetz stirred up the specter of revenge and rage so strongly desired by many victims. Noted psychiatrist Willard Gaylin writes in *The Rage Within: Anger in Modern Life*:

> Most of us endure our frustrations and humiliations without resorting to animal attack. We accept the deprivation without attempting to rectify it by physically attacking either the agent of our deprivation or the fortuitously privileged. The fact that others do not behave in this way is particularly outraging. We are infuriated because we are aware of precisely the same impulses within ourselves which we do not indulge. . . . We are in a rage—those of us who occupy and must use the city streets, because we are aware of our own "right" to feel violent . . . which our self-discipline keeps us from acting out.[8]

Undoubtedly, the Goetz case is the most celebrated mugging case in recent urban history. The possibility that Goetz's situation, the confrontation on a subway, could happen to any New Yorker is obvious. It was the aspect of revenge, the issue of self-defense, and the possession of an illegal handgun that made his case different from others. The case illustrated the difference between taking action, as Bernhard Goetz did, and empathizing with those we identify with, such as Bronson's *Death Wish* character. Nevertheless, the incident itself, which occurred on a New York City subway and was told around the world, reinforced the belief that New York City is indeed a city of violence. Like the crime-victim stories presented here, the Goetz case gave people a vehicle to project their fantasies of revenge against young delinquents who often escape the law. But the fantasies were short-lived once New Yorkers realized that Goetz had overstepped the line demarking appropriate behavior. His status quickly toppled; suddenly, he was portrayed by the media as a lonely eccentric bent on a one-man crusade to eradicate urban crime. As one New Yorker mentioned to me shortly after the incident, "Not only do we have to watch out for muggers like those kids, now we have to watch out for nuts like Goetz!"[9]

In addition to reevaluating the role that crime plays in urban life, the Goetz incident forced other issues: it addressed the question of the quality of life found in an urban setting. Much has been written about the urban scene; its advantages and disadvantages have been scrutinized by sociologists, psychologists, historians, and other culture specialists. The indigenously American cultural theme, that rural life is preferable to urban life, has been one of our strongest cultural myths, pervading our literature, cultural arts, politics, even folklore. More common traits of urban life emphasized by sociologists decades ago, such as alienation, and conservation of energy to prevent psychic overload, are currently being reevaluated. Certain features about city life—for example, the availability of services, the cultural diversity, the stimulating environment, the strong secondary social networks—are regarded today as positive features and even healthy aspects of urban living.[10]

The middle-class New Yorkers I spoke to were consistent in presenting two basic assumptions about living in New York City. These assumptions are the building blocks that make up their urban world view and provide them with "a vision for understanding" the world around them.[11] First, most informants contended that New York is the most dangerous city in the country. They believed that anyone can be a crime victim; no one is immune. Their stories were the testimony to prove this contention.

In addition to seeing it as the major crime city, informants believed New York to be an urban jungle where the social order is continually being disrupted and where dehumanization is a constant state. The crime-victim narrative presents one aspect of urban living. Because of the nature of the topic itself, the world view projected is, to a large degree, fatalistic. The narratives imply that good will towards others in the urban environment is limited, if it exists at all. The urban scene in these stories is full of criminals (ready to maim, murder, rape, and steal), apathetic fellow citizens, and ineffectual police. Despite the melting-pot image commonly associated with New York City, these stories engender a world view which suggests that heterogeneity breeds racism, intolerance, suspicion, and self-denigration. Indeed, in some stories, the teller makes it seem that the victim deserves his fate.

But as there are both negative and positive aspects of urban life, the cynical world view projected by these stories does not present a completely balanced picture. For if New York City were as horrible as informants presented it, it would be an intolerable place to live. Thus, New Yorkers acknowledge the city's cultural and cosmopolitan stature. Native informants are always aware of the city's distinction as a cultural mecca.

While the informants reveal a dangerous world within the personal-experience stories they tell about crime, they balance that cynical world view with a positive, optimistic view of New York City: thus, they could comfortably and without irony call it "the capital of the nation." To them, New York City is a place where any whim can be satisfied at any time.

New Yorkers I spoke with shared some views about their city similar to ones commonly held by many of the over 20 million tourists who visit New York annually. Gerald Handel, in analyzing tourists' expectations of New York City, discovered that visitors not only expect New Yorkers to be unfriendly, but they also feel, as tourists, that they need to be constantly vigilant about crime. Handel notes, "expectations of crime are prominent in the image that visitors had of New York prior to visiting. . . . When asked how New York is different from what they expected, they often reply that there is less crime than they expected or 'I haven't been mugged yet.' "[12] One story collected from the sister of a tourist corroborates Handel's findings:

> This happened to my younger brother's sister-in-law's husband. My brother got married in '65. This must have been about '72. All the years between my brother's wedding, his wife's sister-in-law Alice wanted to come to New York. She wanted to come to New York so bad. And every time she would say something to Sal [her husband], he would say, "Why do you want to go to New York City? You'll just get shot." And that was his stock answer, "You'll just get shot." Finally, Alice persuaded Sal to come to New York. So they packed up the kids, got in the car, and started driving. They drove the 475 miles down from upstate New York onto the West Side Highway. And as they passed the Dyckman Street exit, Sal got shot! . . . This was the time when there was a lot of sniper work going on the Upper West Side. And they deduced that it was a BB. It wasn't heavy action. Someone was fooling around with a rifle and just let go with a shot, and it was almost spent, but it still had enough force. . . . He was hit just below the jawbone. It lodged under his jawbone and had to be removed. So Alice spent the week in New York with my parents, and Sal spent the week in St. Clare's Hospital.
> (M-89)

Sal's experience, which no doubt reinforced his belief that New York City is a dangerous place, was narrated by his sister-in-law, Barbara Fenwick, a native. Sal's belief that people are in constant jeopardy while in New York City underscores a vision of urban life that is implicit in many of the crime-victim stories.

As Sal's story attests, in the world of the crime-victim narrative, there is little regard for the value of human life. The fear that one can unexpectedly come face to face with death infuses these stories with a sense of shock. What informants fear and despise in equal measure is the ubiquity of both gratuitous violence and harm inflicted by offenders without conscience.

As gleaned from these stories, offenders act aggressively in situations and care little for the victim's life. Informants rally against this amorality. Of all the narratives collected for this study, the following one, told to me by Toby Wolf, age sixty, of Brooklyn, reveals most horrifically this disregard for human life:

> This happened about four or five years ago to my cousins. They came back from New York City [to Brooklyn from Manhattan]. It was probably a Saturday night. They parked around the corner from a restaurant. They were thirsty and wanted a drink. Just an ice cream or something like that. They get out of the car, I guess it must have been two blacks. They made my cousins—the man lay down on the floor, and they pulled out his pockets. Took all the keys, wallet, everything. His wife had to give her pocketbook and everything like that.
>
> About three months ago, a friend of theirs who knew the story and knew that he shouldn't resist. . . . They were coming home. I guess to their own house. He was walking down the street, and a colored man pulls out a gun. The wife gives him her pocketbook. The husband remembers about my cousin emptying his pockets. So, he put his hand in his pocket to take out his wallet, and they was standing there with the gun in his stomach. And as the man saw him stick his hand in this pocket, he shot him through the stomach. He killed him. He didn't die immediately. He was in the hospital, and then he died. **(M-26)**

When Toby Wolf told the story, she was visibly shaken; her voice quivered, and its shrill tone convincingly disclosed her anguish and frustration about both incidents, particularly the senseless death of her cousins' friends. When she came to the second part of the story, the second mugging, she said emphatically, with a sense of determination and anger, that the friend "knew that he shouldn't resist." That the man followed the rules by starting to hand over his wallet to the mugger, and that his submissive actions were misinterpreted by an impulsive mugger, who killed him, made the event and the story more shocking and frightening. Not only does the story present the second victim's compliance to avoid harm, but the victim's action, reaching into his pocket for his money, seemed to the audience to be an appropriate way for him to have dealt with such a perilous situation. It seems, too, that in Wolf's telling, the first victimization pales in comparison to the second. In Wolf's narrative, however, it is clear how such a dramatic tale imparts street smarts to future victims. That the lesson fails in this particular case is an unusual enough circumstance for it to serve as the compelling dramatic point of the tale.

One aspect of the world view that informants present in these stories deals with the portrayal of violence. Offenders were presented as thriving on gratuitous violence, which was both disturbing and incomprehensible to many informants. The short narrative below is one of many examples:

> A friend of mine who is a woman in her late fifties . . . was in the elevator and got caught in the elevator with some man that walked in at the last minute, and [he] beat her up very badly. He didn't want anything. He just came in to do as much damage as he could. (M-30)

Other stories previously mentioned, including the story about the young man who was murdered at a stoplight, and the one about the woman who was murdered and dismembered by the elevator operator, exemplify a world where criminal violence is both unpredictable and unacceptable, where the social order seems to be continually disrupted by violence, and where victims and potential victims believe themselves to be without protection or recourse.

In these stories, the urban world is presented as a world without emotion, remorse, or conscience, especially in view of the offender's actions. "He didn't want anything. He just came in to do as much damage as he could," a comment culled from the last story, represents informants' typical opinions of offenders. This lack of conscience, particularly in juvenile offenders, has been discussed by Charles E. Silberman in his exhaustive study on criminal violence. He writes, "In the past, juveniles who exploded in violence tended to feel considerable guilt or remorse afterwards; the new criminals have been so brutalized in their own up-bringing that they seem incapable of viewing their victims as fellow human beings, or of realizing that they have killed another person."[13] It is not only this lack of emotion or the display of violence that informants deplore; they find the offender's complete disregard for fellow humans incomprehensible. Some informants, however, seem to have become hardened by a lack of concern towards victims.

Urbanites try to come to some understanding of these events. The very act of telling these stories is an important way for narrators to work out a meaning for them. Stories help New Yorkers and others attempt to understand how violence and urban crime affect them and others in their social network, and to allow them a chance to work out a meaning for these extraordinary events in a collaborative way.

In many cases, when a narrator tells the story of another victim, he or she is using the victim's experiences to devise meaning for him- or herself. For example, when Toby Wolf told the story previously cited, she was trying to understand in her anguish how such an awful event could have occurred; and like other narrators and victims, she could find no satisfactory answer.

The use of these crime-victim stories vis à vis the world view they present is related to the work of Richard Sennett. In his work on social identity and city life, Sennett postulates how adolescents derive meaning from the experiences of others and, as a result, isolate themselves from experience in general. He writes,

> By imagining the meaning of a class of experiences in advance or apart from living them, a young person is freed from having to go through the experience itself to understand its meaning. He makes up the meaning in isolation. . . . If projection of the meaning of experience does work as a stable substitute, then the young person has actually acquired a powerful weapon to prevent any exposure of himself; in other words, he has learned how to insulate himself in advance from experiences that might portend dislocation and disorder.[14]

Sennett continues by saying that an adolescent can then create "a purified picture of his own identity," and by doing so can eradicate from his world view "disorder and painful disruption from conscious consideration."[15]

In other words, if one hears the story of a victim, one can determine what meaning that experience holds without being victimized; knowing about victimization thus permits isolation. For that reason, it is understandable why some, though few, informants I spoke to seemed unaffected by crime-victim events. More important, this premise shows how crime-victim stories function as a mechanism whereby one learns about a specific type of unpleasant (to say the least) urban experience. As a result of this isolation, urbanites need not take responsibility for finding solutions for reducing the urban crime rate, such as reporting an incident to the police or joining a neighborhood crime-watch patrol.

In some ways, the urbanites I spoke with acted similarly to Sennett's adolescents. By assuming that the social order is continually being disrupted by crime, city dwellers can use the experiences revealed in the stories to project order and meaning onto the world. As a result, it then is axiomatic that one cannot ride the subway without fear, or feel safe walking down a dimly lit street at night, or leave one's home even for a few minutes without fear of burglary:

> Well, I got robbed in my apartment last summer. . . . It was in a very nice Hispanic neighborhood. And there were welfare people living next door. But my building was really nice; mostly actors and students. And it was totally white, too. I don't know if that makes a difference, but there had been a rash of robberies that month. I went out for about twenty minutes and I came back, and the door was unlocked. "And my small appliances and jewelry was gone. . . . I felt really rotten, and a little frightened. Pissed me off because it took the police an hour and a half to show up! . . .[16]

Because urbanites are so inundated by these crime-victim events, in both popular and folk culture, they find it difficult to account for and understand gratuitous violence.

Narrators projected a world characterized by an intolerance of others. This intolerance not only is based on features of urban life, such as density, incivility, or dehumanization; it is also based on prejudice. In the world of the crime-victim story, heterogeneity in New York breeds antagonism toward others. Most often, white narrators and listeners covertly express negative attitudes toward different ethnic and racial groups. One of the functions of the crime-victim narrative is to allow the teller to communicate such negative feelings by incorporating ethnic slurs or stereotypical portrayals of offenders and, occasionally, of victims.

> Last year or two years ago on Passover, they [relatives] opened the door for Eliahu, and three gunmen walked in to rob them . . . they robbed them. They got everybody down, and one woman got to the bedroom . . . and she called the police. The police came while the gunmen were still there. . . . They had a shootout and killed the robber. . . . This was on Ninety-fifth Street and Amsterdam Avenue. We were kidding around at the dinner table, and my aunt said, "Don't open the door for Eliahu because Puerto Ricans will come in!"[17]

Most often, crime-victim story narrators, the majority of whom are white, identify offenders by race. "A black kid, you know, did this," or "Two blacks came up to me and put a knife in my side," or "He was Hispanic, no shirt." Narrators frequently use the word *they* to characterize groups: "They get their guns out too often" or "They just want to harm you" are ways in which evidence of prejudice appears in stories:

> You remember when everybody was here. . . . and I saw the nigger in the window. . . . That's why I never put my shade down, because I see who was stealing. I came over to here [to the kitchen window], and he [her husband] says to me, "Someday, you're gonna get a gun to your head . . . if you don't mind your own business. . . ." But I heard a noise. I says [to a black male outside of her window], "Hey, what are you doin' out in the window over there?" . . . With the cap and the sneakers. Big nigger! He jumped from the window on to the top of the roof . . . [then] he goes up the fire escape.[18]

In the following example, several themes appear: the unpredictability of crime, the belief that the police are ineffective in preventing crime, and the characterization of the offender as a "nice black boy."

> I know my mother was mugged. Yeah. This was about eight years ago when I first moved out. She was coming home from bingo. My mother, the bingo maven. Did not win that night. So she had a few dollars and her bingo chips and dotters and all the crap that she keeps. And P.S. this kid comes over.

She said he was about sixteen years old. Nice black boy [sarcastic]. And as she was putting the key in the door, the front entrance, he pushed her and tried to grab her bag. My mother started screaming. He knocked her down. She didn't really get hurt. She hurt her knees because she fell on her knees. She got knocked down. He grabbed her bingo bag. And she went running upstairs. She was very upset, to say the least. I said, "Did you win that night?" She said, "Maybe I had two dollars in the bag. He's gonna find a lot of crap!" I said, "Did you call the police?"—"What for? What are they gonna do?" I said, "You should report it anyway just because it should be reported. Can you describe the guy?" "Sure, I can describe the guy, but what good is it gonna do?" You know, the apathetic thing and doesn't want to get involved and all that nonsense. She never saw the kid again in the neighborhood. And she moved right after that. "That's it, I can't take it any more." She was really frightened. . . . (**M-69**)

Unfortunately, the urban world view these stories reveal is a world where interracial harmony is unachievable. Narrators reinforce prejudice by using racial slurs throughout the stories, by lacing the stories with editorial comments and asides, or by harping on negative racial stereotypes. The use of folk narrative to display racial prejudices is not new to the study of folklore.

Folklorists and cultural historians who have studied the Afro-American folk tale, and specifically the trickster tale, have discussed how these narratives have been used within Afro-American culture. In the trickster tale, the slave often pokes fun at his master to get the upper hand in a difficult situation. The white slave master usually demands that the black slave perform some action, or be the butt of some joke. However, in the story, the master is often duped by the slave, who ultimately exerts some control, however covert, over him.[19] The observations made about the Afro-American trickster tale show that character traits such as deceitfulness and trickery were successful ways to avoid physical or mental cruelty. By being shrewd and clever, the black slave could attempt to control his world, if only in narrative form, and achieve some sense of self-worth. As Lawrence Levine and others have also pointed out, slave narratives reinforced the black fear of white power. Thus, trickster tales were a constant reminder of how such power could be undermined.[20]

Have the tables turned? Are whites now using crime-victim stories in the same fashion that blacks used trickster tales? While it is only conjecture, this intriguing question is worth considering. Several informants implied that they held animosity towards blacks and/or Hispanics. "They always get out their guns" seemed to be a euphemism for "blacks," whom many whites stereotyped as invariably armed or into creating trouble. Of course, like most stereotypes, these generalizations are absurd. Yet in the world view of the crime-victim story, there seemed little room for ambiguities: the Goetz shooting simply reinforced their perception.

The Afro-American trickster tale, a shield against hatred and discrimination, has been replaced today by Afro-American forms that present and promote black pride. But for whites, the situation has changed. If what Charles Silberman writes is true—that whites *fear* the very presence of blacks—then is it not plausible that crime-victim stories told by whites express hostility toward blacks, and particularly a fear of young black males, who statistically are in the highest offender group? The supposition that crime-victim narratives are now used as a covert way to both express and shield race hatred and fear by whites toward blacks, just as blacks used trickster tales to express opinions against whites, indicates how groups still use and manipulate expressive narrative forms to deal with situations in which they feel powerless. The plight of the slave in the antebellum South and the white man on the Times Square street corner are obviously too incongruous to compare. But what is being suggested is that we need to pay attention to how any group that feels powerless (for complex historical and economic reasons, or because of what is perceived as an insolvable urban problem) can creatively manipulate a narrative form to express, no matter how covertly or how unflatteringly, their point of view.

Informants, then, present a dualistic world view. On one hand, they assume New York City to be unsafe; yet, on the other, they expect it to be a cultural paradise. While most informants viewed New York as the city of Gotham, others reminded me that it is a "fun town," a city that never sleeps, a city unlike any other in the world. Both components of this world view are needed for urbanites to have a coherent, balanced view of their urban world.

A final component of this world view deals with how some informants view the world in general, as fair or unfair, just or unjust. Many victims not only feel powerless in their situations, but they also feel that they, too, are somehow to blame. To control their fear, and to provide a rationale for being victimized at random, many stated that they were "in the wrong place at the wrong time." And on occasion, informants said that some victims "got what they deserved." These views are consistent with the ideas of Melvin J. Lerner, who coined the term the *just world hypothesis* to describe his theory that victims are often seen as getting their just rewards. This is especially true when nonvictims cannot project themselves into the victim's situation:

> Individuals have a need to believe that they live in a world where people generally get what they deserve. The belief that the world is just enables the individual to confront his physical and social environment as though they were stable and orderly. Without such a belief it would be difficult for the individual to commit himself to the pursuit of long range goals or even to the socially regulated behavior of day-to-day life. Since the belief that the

world is just serves such an important adaptive function for the individual, people are very reluctant to give up this belief, and they can be greatly troubled if they encounter evidence that suggests that the world is not really just or orderly at all.

The justness of others' fate thus has clear implications for the future of the individual's own fate. If others can suffer unjustly, then the individual must admit to the unsettling prospect that he too can suffer unjustly. As a consequence of the perceived interdependence between their own fate and the fate of others in their environment, individuals confronted with an injustice generally will be motivated to restore justice. One way of accomplishing this is by acting to compensate the victim; another is by persuading oneself that the victim deserves to suffer.[21]

Lerner's "just world hypothesis" clearly relates to the telling of these crime-victim stories. The stories present two distinct views of the city world. The first is the ideal of the just world that tellers would like to believe exists, where neighbors help each other, people help victims, and property and life are respected, as well as personal space and possessions. Narrators present this ideal world *outside* of their stories, a world that they wish existed. But in the unjust world *within* these stories, property is taken without consent, policemen are incapable of providing assistance, and bystanders don't give a damn. Once the victim is compensated, even by being listened to empathetically, or the victim is blamed, the stories then can become a vehicle for restoring order and justice in the victim's, potential victim's, narrator's, or listener's perspective. They permit urbanites to convince themselves that the world is still safe. Not only do they function in this manner, but the telling of these personal-experience stories also creates a constantly re-forming folk group based on the common factor of crime victimization. These stories are conversational icebreakers and allow for instant expressions of empathy and camaraderie between tellers and listeners who share the world view that crime victimization is a major feature of city life, or who have been victimized. As Roger Abrahams has noted, the sharing of personal-experience stories allows us to engage with others "with whom we have never otherwise had a relationship."[22] Crime-victim stories shared with fellow urbanites thus create, sustain, and reinforce a sense of community between victims. One needs only to arrive late at a party after being mugged and be regaled with similar experiences told by those present. Whether the victim knew the tellers or not prior to the party is inconsequential.

The basic assumptions that form an urban world culled from these narratives about city life are far from new: density, heterogeneity, cosmopolitanism, alienation, and disregard for others are well-documented features of the urban environment. What is of issue and concern is the relationship between a narrative expressive form, the crime-victim narrative, and these features of urban life. Certainly, the crime-victim narrative is a product of the urban environment; it discusses a distinct problem that affects the quality of life of most city dwellers. Most important, it is a product created by urbanites themselves to address the vexing problem of crime, which has baffled urban planners, law enforcers, and city bureaucrats. The crime-victim story is an ingenious way for city people to attempt to express their concerns about victimization, independently from the authorities, whose role is to study urban crime, enact laws, and effect change. The vitality and energy of urbanites, here New Yorkers, has resulted in the creation, transmission, and utilization of a specific type of personal-experience narrative, the crime-victim story. This type of personal narrative expresses the fears, concerns, and values that are important to those who lead an urban life. The crime-victim story, replete with its own themes, character types, and functions, and instilled with values for everyday living, proves that people respond in creative, innovative, and yet traditional ways in order to understand the world around them. The urban crime situation is perceived as so overwhelming by many people I spoke to, that the telling of the crime-victim story allows them to humanize the problem, reduce a nebulous fear of crime, and attempt to gain some control over their lives and actions.

At first glance, it may seem that the negative features of urban life discussed here work against the idea of the crime-victim story as a creative expression of urban folklore. But that is not the case. The crime-victim story is an expressive response, on a folk level, of integrating an urban problem with a traditional solution. While it may seem that everyone in New York "just gets shot," as Sal, the tourist victim, would probably try to convince us, these conceptualizations about the urban environment, regardless of how negative they appear at first, are manipulated into powerful images and shaped into a structured story. The city dwellers I spoke with have creatively manipulated these urban events and experiences into a forceful and traditional story about urban crime and victimization, often unknowingly contributing to a rich source of folklore and traditional expression in the urban environment.

Appendix

M-1   Bags on the Curb
Ruth Melberg, June 13, 1977
See chapter 2.

M-2   The Apartment Sale I
Ruth Melberg, June 13, 1977

There was a middle-aged couple living in our house who had a big six-room apartment, and they had bought a condominium in Florida, and they had a lot of furniture and odds and ends and things in their house. They advertised in the paper that over the weekend they were selling photographic equipment, and cameras, china, typewriters, and odds and ends at a reasonable price. So the first weekend, they had quite a few people that bought a lot of stuff, but they still had a lot of stuff left over, and they decided that they would, since they were so successful the first weekend, they would do it a second weekend. I warned them not to do it because I told them you don't know who was coming into your house. But she claimed that such lovely people came in that nothing could happen. Well, anyway, they put the ad in the newspaper the following week.

In the afternoon, a lot of people came up to their place. Sure enough, a man and his son came up and looked around and said that they were very interested in buying a set of golf clubs and a typewriter. "How much would it be?" And I think it was quoted about $125. So the man says he didn't have enough money with him, but could he come back later in the afternoon? He says, "Well, what time will you be here?" He says, "Well, we have a dinner appointment at six," he says, "I'd like to finish here at the latest a quarter to six." The man said, "Oh, I'll be back before then." So he said, "All right, I'll hold it for you." Sure enough, about five-thirty this man and his son came back to buy the golf clubs and whatever else it was that they were interested in. But the wife knew that her friends were waiting downstairs to go out for dinner. And he said, "Okay." So she went downstairs, and she saw that it was taking a long time. So she decided to go up and call him. So she goes upstairs to her floor, and she puts the key in the door, and just as she opened the door, her husband yells, "Julia, don't come in here, they're holding me up!" And with that, the man grabbed her and pulled her into the house. She sees her husband with a terrible gash over his forehead. They tied up both the husband and the wife and threw them on the bed, and they ransacked the house, and then they just opened the door and left very quietly by the elevator. Nobody realized what was going on. The friends were downstairs waiting for a long time, and finally they decided they would go up and find out. So when they went upstairs, the husband had managed to loosen his hands so that when they rang the bell, he was yelling for help. So they started pounding on the door. When he opened the door, they saw that he was bleeding badly, and they ran for help. They called the police. That was another incident of people being fooled by letting strangers into their house. After that incident, they didn't bother advertising anymore. They called a second-hand furniture dealer, who bought everything at one time, and they didn't have to worry about being held up anymore.

M-2   The Apartment Sale II
Ruth Melberg, January 12, 1981

This woman had a three-bedroom apartment. It was a three-bedroom apartment, and she was quite comfortable. And she had beautiful stuff in her living room and foyer, etc. And they were going to Florida, and she didn't want to take all the stuff, so she put an ad in the newspaper. And I warned her not to do it because she never knows who will come up. But she insisted that was the only way to do it. So she put the ad in the newspaper.

People were trekking in and out, and she was selling stuff little by little. And around three o'clock in the afternoon, this very lovely black man and his son come up, and they look around and pick out certain items. And they told them that they didn't bring money with them and they would be back around five o'clock and pay him. And they should set out this stuff on the side. And the man said, "Fine."

So around five-fifteen they had a dinner appointment. So this man and his son show up around five-fifteen. The wife was a little annoyed because they came fifteen minutes late. And the people they were going out to dinner with were downstairs waiting. So the wife said, "I'll wait for you downstairs, hurry up." So he said, "Okay."

With that she left the house, and the black man pulls a gun on the owner of the apartment. He was terribly frightened. And they started putting things they wanted in a bag of some sort. It took time, because they eventually wanted to tie him up, and they wanted to go through the whole apartment to see if they got everything.

His wife was downstairs waiting. She sees it's taking an awfully long time. So she decided she would go back upstairs to her husband to see what was taking so long. With that she puts the key in the door, she opens the door, she hears her husband yell, "Don't come in!" But by then the door had opened, and they grabbed her in. And they tied her up, and they put masking tape over her mouth. Hit the husband over the head with the gun. They opened his head. They took what they wanted and they left.

The people they were to have dinner with saw it was taking so long, so they came up, and when they came up and saw the door wasn't completely closed. And they came in, and they found the couple tied and bound. Their mouths were taped. They took him to the hospital. He had a couple of stitches in his head. And they never found out who did it. That's the story.

M-3   Just Her Imagination
Robert Ross, June 23, 1977
See Introduction.

M-4   Keeping Your Glasses On
Stanley Wolman, July 17, 1977

I was coming out of the subway station, and it was in the middle of the day, about 1:00 P.M. Oh, I guess it wasn't in the spring, because it was pretty cold out. I remember that. And I just had come from the doctor. I had some kind of examination, which kind of left me spaced out. I was carrying my school books, and as I got halfway up the stairs . . . I was the last person out of the train, so I was moving kind of slow . . . or I seemed to be the last person in a stream of people. I remember there was this lady in a mink coat ahead of me. She just walked up the stairs. And I noticed there was this bunch of kids up the stairs, and it was about halfway up. Apparently it was a trap, and then I heard them say, "Let's get this dude. Hey, let's get this dude." And they came from both sides of the stairs. So I was trapped on the stairs. And I had this thought . . . which was really a stupid thought to have at a time when you are about to be possibly seriously injured. But they didn't have weapons or anything. That was what the police said. There were probably ten of them or something like that . . . male and female. They were all black. The one they caught was sixteen . . . so I guess they were around that age. I just struggled down the stairs. They came from both sides. Somehow I kept my feet. I must have started fighting without thinking . . . like an animal. I kept my feet to the bottom of the stairs, and I remember getting smashed in the face and falling down. And somebody ran and got the cops. I don't know how long the whole thing took. It didn't seem that long. I don't remember too well. I know that I was fighting for a while. I remember staggering away, and then I remember getting kicked a little bit. I remember swinging around and smashing someone in the face really hard—it was definitely the best punch I threw! Unfortunately, it was a cop who was just trying to catch me as I was stumbling away. So then he said something like, "You stupid motherfucker," and pinned me to the wall. He realized that I was totally spaced out and had no idea what was happening.

They caught one. I remember all the kids standing around. I remember the kids walking around, and I was really scared. I was more scared than when I was being beaten up. There were these people staring. The kids were saying things like, "You'd better not press charges, or else we're gonna get you," 'cause they knew that one of their friends got caught . . . they caught one kid. Of course, my glasses were knocked off. I had no idea what was happening because I couldn't see anything. . . .

M-5 Locked-Up Grandma
Stanley Wolman, July 17, 1977

I'm sure I've heard some stories. Oh, yeah, my aunt has a loft on West Seventeenth Street. My grandmother comes over a lot. She comes over to see them once in a while. And she was in the basement, and these two guys came down there while she was taking laundry out of the basement. They robbed her. They didn't physically hurt her. They tied her up and put and locked her in a closet in the basement. And, ah . . . she was there for a couple of hours before my aunt came down and heard her. And, ah . . . that was a traumatic experience for her.

M-6 A Put-Up Job
Rose Lefferts, June 13, 1977

A blond woman was walking along Atlantic Avenue, and two fellas came along on bicycles and they robbed her. But they caught the fella. And then a friend let me out on Maple Street and said that she had gone to cash her check and two fellas had robbed her. They followed her. You understand me exactly? Looked like a put-up job. Two men followed that bitch when she went to cash her check. You understand me? How do you know where somebody is going unless somebody tells you . . . so it's a put-up job . . . and they took $190 off of her.

M-7 Fireworks at Coney Island
Barry Melberg, June 13, 1977

Every Tuesday, my friend and I, and really a whole bunch of us, went to the [Coney Island] boardwalk just to watch the fireworks. I was coming back with my friend, and we were listening to the radio. Basically all that happened was that we saw about six or seven kids behind us. So there were six or seven guys behind us, and they quickly surrounded us and started hitting us. I got hit in the back of the head, and the radio flew out of my hand. My friend started getting beaten up, and after they had their fun—and they were Puerto Rican; we heard them speaking Spanish—after they had their fun, they left. I wound up with a fat lip and some sore ribs. My friend had a bloody nose. I mean, it wasn't really anything bad; it was pure sport. It was just like a Tuesday night out-on-the-town type of thing, and who can we find to beat up. I don't know if it mattered if we were white, black, yellow, or whatever.

M-8 The Crying Mugger
Maria Diaz, June 3, 1977

My mother was going to church that night, and she was going to church, right? She had one dollar, and it was for the offering. That's all she had on her. One dollar. We used to live right by the church, and she was walking down to it. And this big guy comes up to her with a knife on her. He says, "Give me your money!" And my mother gives him the dollar. My mother looked at him, and he started crying. He started crying! This was something spiritual. The Sister said that she was praying for my mother because she felt my mother was in danger. It must have been that God was protecting her then and there, and softened the guy's heart. Then instead of mugging her, he gave my mother back the dollar.

M-9 Broke Like Spaghetti
Susan Roberts, June 17, 1977
See chapter 2.

M-10 Just Been Mugged
Pamela Day, March 17, 1978
See chapter 1.

M-11 Buying a Newspaper
Ruth Melberg, June 13, 1977
See Introduction; chapter 4.

M-12 The Fifth Floor
Ruth Melberg, March 20, 1976
See chapter 2.

M-13 The Baby Carriage
Susan Weiss, June 4, 1977

And there was a girl with a baby carriage, a stroller kind of carriage. And somebody came along and pushed the kid, and the mother ran for the kid; they grabbed her bag and left. The girl was hysterical.

M-14   Run, John, Run
Ruth Melberg, July 13, 1979

My nephew and his friend—my nephew is fifteen years old, and his friend is the same age—took two young little girls to the movies and got out about nine o'clock. They walked the girls to their homes. The girls lived in the same apartment house, and they brought the girls to their doors and then came down. And they started walking toward the bus. It must have taken about a half a block when about six boys pounced on them. The friend was so frightened that he started to run, and he called to John, "Run, John, run!" He saw these boys behind them. The two of them started running, and these boys ran after them. But the friend was able to run faster, and they caught John, and they started beating him up, and they put a gash in his head—about eight or nine stitches. And they took off his wristwatch and took out all his money. They ripped his clothes. And the girl's father saw this from the window, and he started running down, but when he got downstairs the boys were gone. He called an ambulance, and they took John to the hospital, and they stitched up his head. They suggested that he stay overnight because there was the possibility of a concussion. And he stayed overnight, and then his mother wanted him to come home. So the doctor says, "Well, take him home, but he must stay in bed for a week and be very quiet." Which is what he did. It was reported to the police. And the police came and asked a lot of questions, and John answered as best as he could. His friend answered as best as he could. As the policeman said, "It's very difficult to catch these boys."

M-15   Twice in One Day
Doris Connelly, June 16, 1977

He was working in the heart of Harlem. It was like Lexington [Avenue] and 135th [Street] or something like that, in a Headstart Program. He was really a smart kid, extremely intelligent, but he just looked like a normal Brooklyn kid. Every day he would walk to work through Morningside Park. I said to him, "Bob, please. . ." He had done this for six weeks. I said to him one day, "It's making me crazy that you're walking through the park every day. So why don't you at least go on the street. Make it quick and take the other way round." He says, "Yeah, I guess you're right." He never thinks about getting hurt. He's very political. If someone ripped him off he would probably think, "They need it more than I do." He's very conscious of that. This kid is very pure of heart.

So he said, "Well, I guess you're right." I think what I did was instill a little bit of fear in him, because he hadn't even thought about it before then. The next day he came home, and he was a total wreck. He was a nervous wreck. "Bob, what's wrong with you?" He said, "Well, I figured I'd be safe and walk through the city coming home." It was four-thirty in the afternoon. Two guys came up to him and pulled a gun to his back. One of them pulled his arm around and said like this, "Hey, buddy, got a quarter or something?" And Bob turned to him, and when he looked back in the other direction, there was a guy on the other side with a gun in his coat. And he said, "Don't say a word. Just come with me." They pushed him down an alley and took all his money. Took everything out of his wallet, and he had just gone to the Apollo to get tickets for the Temptations. No one who's white goes to the Apollo Theatre. That's another thing. He didn't even think of that. So, they took his tickets. Then they let him go. Another five minutes later, another guy stops him and pulls a knife on him. So Bob goes . . . he was so upset he started yelling at this guy, "Fucker, leave me alone. I just got ripped off five minutes ago.

You're not going to take anything else from me!" No one in their right mind would have yelled at someone like that. He just started screaming. So he [the robber] goes, "Okay, man, cool, cool, cool!" [timid tone] And Bob came home, and he said, "I don't care about the money, but the tickets for the Temptations are all sold out now!" [laughs]

M-16   The Visit to the Doctor
Bernadette Potter, June 16, 1977

A couple of years ago, I went to my doctor's office because I had a nervous stomach. He and I were inside in his little room, and there's an office outside. And we heard someone creaking on the floor. The office has these old wooden floors outside, and so we just figured someone was upstairs walking around. So, ah, he opened the door, and there are these guys there, and one has a gun. And one says, "All right, get back into the room!" And interestingly enough, I had paid the doctor by check, which I usually don't do, and I had fifty dollars in cash in my bag, but I just dropped my pocketbook in my nervousness. We went inside. And they went for the doctor's money. They figured maybe he had a lot. He had mainly checks. They took his money, took the money out, and this is the weird part—there was about ten seconds when all of us just stood there and looked at each other. And this little one, the little one with the gun, nervous type, he thought he probably was James Cagney, he says, "Let's put them away!" Right? The other one said, "NO, MAN, let's just get the hell out of here." They didn't touch my pocketbook outside. They just left.

The doctor and I were like this [trembling hands]. He started talking about [starts to laugh] . . . he really went off the deep end. He really did. He started talking about . . . the two guys were black and about seventeen and eighteen for the most part . . . and he started talking about how he was always helping the colored people in the neighborhood, and why should this happen to him.

So the police came, and they questioned us and all that. We did everything right, 'cause I said, "Let's call the police." I didn't realize that he was still bent out of shape until afterwards when the police came. And he just . . . [nervous laughter] . . . I went home by myself on the subway. I guess I looked green because I remember trembling, holding the pole with both hands, and everyone in the car was staring at me. I guess I looked weird. I went home. I fixed myself a big rum-and-coke and then called my family and told them what happened. And that was the end of that. I was so willing to help the police. I gave the police my name and address, telephone number, and all that, and they never called me for identification. That was the last time I saw that doctor!

M-17   Robbed Twice
Robert Ross, June 2, 1977

Well, my brother was robbed twice in the same park. It was when he was going to Columbia [University] near Morningside Park. . . . Both times it was kids that were about twelve years old. It was a bunch of them. And they asked him for money. And he'd give them a little money. . . . They just said, "Give me all the money you have in your pocket and your change." I'm trying to think if they had a knife. I think one of them may have had a knife. It happened both times in the same park. And then he ended up not walking through the park, because he used to walk through there from the subway. . . . This was in the late sixties. He decided not to walk through there anymore. It has a bad reputation. In fact, the same thing happened to me in that park with young kids at about the same time in the sixties. And the same thing happened to me. . . . They asked for money. A few kids . . . like two or three of them that were in the park. YEAH! That's the one! That park is something of a legend in that area. There's a majority of people who won't have anything to do with that park. They claim to have been chased or robbed there.

M-18   Held at Knifepoint
Mark Nathansen, June 22, 1977

My father was held at knifepoint early in July. My father was a peddler. And he wandered around the city and sold a lot of stuff on Second Avenue, way over on the Lower East Side, the East Bronx and Harlem. . . . He sold anything he liked to . . . mostly clothing . . . anything like that . . . bric-a-brac . . . knick-knacks and stuff. Oh, anything he knew of he bought . . . and, uh, he had some stories . . . he was sort of taunted and chased by hoodlum kids if he was carrying his bags to the corner. He was called Santa Claus and other names. Once he was in Harlem on 125th Street. He went into a store on 125th Street. He used to go there fairly regularly. And it was in the winter, and two thugs grabbed him, shoved him against a wall, held a knife to him, and stripped him . . . you know . . . took his wallet.

M-19   Just off Fifth Avenue
Joe Bowers, June 19, 1977

What happened was I was over visiting a friend down in the Village; down in Greenwich Village. It was on East Eleventh Street just off Fifth Avenue. I'd been visiting my friend. We were watching television that night, and it got to be about 1:30 A.M., and I got up to go home. I was just walking down the street going to the IRT subway to catch my train to go home. I was walking down the street. I wasn't paying attention to anybody. I was kind of watching the sidewalk, because you have to in New York because of all the dogs. Anyway, so I was walking down the street, and I wasn't paying attention to what was going on around me.

I noticed that there was a man coming down the sidewalk towards me. He was on the same side of the sidwalk as I was. So I took a step, you know, to the left, so I could or that we wouldn't run into each other. And I just kept on going. And . . . but he got close to me. All of a sudden, he jumped in front of me into my path. He had a club in one hand and a knife in the other. And he says, "Don't say anything, just give me your money." And I said, "Sure, here." And I just reached into my pocket, and I handed him the money, and he goes, "Give me all of it!" I said, "Sure." And I reached into my pocket—I had over some pennies and change. I gave him the pennies and said, "There it is, that's everything." He goes, "Okay, give me your watch!" And I said, "Here, sure. There you go." And then he said, "All right, now, just keep going and don't look back." I said, "Okay, goodnight." And just kept right on going. I had a subway token in the other pocket—that I didn't give him. I wanted to get home.

M-20   Well, They Got Her
Bernadette Potter, June 16, 1977
See chapter 2.

M-21 Police Academy
Bernadette Potter, June 16, 1977
See chapter 3.

M-22 Washington Square Park
Jill Polin, June 4, 1977

Crime, knifings, muggings . . . there was a story about a mugging. A couple was walking through Washington Square Park, and they were robbed at knifepoint by muggers. They told the police what happened. And they walked a little further and they got mugged again, I think by the same muggers.

M-23 A Big Mistake
Ellen Schwartz, July 19, 1977

Well, I was mugged on Thirtieth Street and Eighth Avenue in my boyfriend's building elevator. . . . I got out of the bus around seven-fifteen, and this little boy said to me, "Hmm, it's already dark." It was January. I thought maybe I should call Tom from Penn Station and have him walk me home. I was in a very good mood. That is always a liability in New York. I thought it was ridiculous! It was only seven-fifteen at night. This is absurd. And so I walked home, and all the way home I had this weird feeling that something was going to happen. And sure enough, it did.

So after I turned the corner on Thirtieth Street and Eighth Avenue, I see this guy lurking under the awning of Tom's building. And then again, I thought to myself, "Humm, watch out!" And then again, I felt in a good mood—"Don't be silly!" Uhm, so again, I didn't listen [to myself]. I thought, "Oh, that's ridiculous, you know. Can't be afraid of everybody."

As I approached the building, he kept standing under the awning. And he paused—a little trick that I had never known before—and he calls up to a friend in the building and he says, "Hey, I'll be right up."

I had never heard of this trick before, and I fell for it as if he really was visiting somebody in the building. So I walked into the vestibule, and I go to buzz Tom, and he walked in behind me when Tom buzzed me back. And when Tom buzzed me back, I walked in. Normally, 99.44% of the time, I slam the door behind me and tell them behind me that "I'm sorry, but I can't let you in." But I was in a good mood, and I let him slip in behind me, and at that moment I realized that I had made a big mistake. And the elevator was standing open in the lobby, and I raced over to it. I was considerably ahead of him—"I'll race to the elevator and close the door before he can get in," I thought to myself. And I almost got away with it. But as the door was closing, it was open about three to four inches. He stuck his arm in and forced the door back, and I knew that I shouldn't have done that. And he got in the elevator, and I pressed seven and he pressed two. I knew the building, and I knew that two was only one flight up. As soon as the door closed he said, "Listen, lady, give me all your money." And I said, "What?" And he said, "Give me all your money!" And I said, "Oh, you've got to be joking." And he said, "No, no, I'm not kidding." And I said, "I really don't find this amusing, please, this is not the time to be fooling around. I don't find this very funny, please cut the comedy." That may have been very stupid of me, because he could have freaked out on me. So we had this discussion whether or not he was serious. He finally pulled this butter knife out of his pocket. It was like a mustard knife that he must have stolen from the corner deli or something. And I said, "You must be kidding." So I looked at it and said, "OH!" and at that point we reached the second floor. It was only one flight up, and the doors opened. And he still wanted to have my money; we were still negotiating. So the door opened automatically, and he came at me with his hand and tried to clap his hand around my mouth, saying, "Now, don't scream." And I said to myself, "Oh, what an excellent idea." So I let out with an incredible howl, my Brooklyn coloratura. He fled. He ran away.

And I was also really angry. It was Friday night, and I just had been paid. I had cashed my pay check, and I had fifty dollars on me. Now I realize it was insanity, I would have given it to him—everything that I had and write a check for more. That was six years ago, and I was young and foolish, and times were not quite as critical as they are now . . . and anyway he ran away, and not a soul came out of their apartments.

M-24   I Want It Now
　　　　 Norma Schultz, August 20, 1978
　　　　 See chapter 2.

M-25   The Elevator
　　　　 Toby Wolf, August 20, 1978

Incidentally, did your mother tell you about the woman who was robbed in the elevator? This is what I understand. Two women got in the elevator. I think one was with a child. One lived on the fifth floor, and one lived on the sixth floor. Evidently, a young fellow walked in at the same time, and the woman on the fifth floor got off. And as soon as the door closed, he took out a knife and held it to the woman's throat. He goes for her jewelry and her things. He didn't hurt her. So be careful!

M-26   My Cousin
　　　　 Toby Wolf, August 20, 1978
　　　　 See chapter 5.

M-27   Hunting Knives
　　　　 Marvin Woltz, November 26, 1977
　　　　 See chapter 2.

M-28   We Didn't Stop
　　　　 Marvin Woltz, November 26, 1977

I was going to a concert in the city with my friends and saw this guy being mugged, but we didn't stop. We would have been late for the concert. I can't say that. But we didn't stop, and that's the truth. I don't know if we would have stopped if we hadn't been late or that's just a good excuse. Maybe we wouldn't have stopped. Just a guy getting beat up on the street corner. But it's kind of scary to stop and help when there are so many people who are armed.

M-29   Bike Tour
　　　　 Robert Ross, June 13, 1977
　　　　 See chapter 4.

M-30   The Elevator
Ruth Melberg, March 20, 1976
See chapter 5.

M-31   South Jamaica
Marvin Woltz, November 26, 1977

This is a weird story. You know that Rochdale is a co-op. It's just on the edge of South Jamaica. It was really good when it started. It was supposed to be really nice 'cause it's near St. Albans. My friend's cousin . . . he's a gym teacher, well, anyway, he came home one night about five o'clock, and he got out of his car, and he got stabbed by a black guy. And then . . . it just mitigates hating people . . . minority groups . . . and he was stabbed by a black guy. But then a second guy comes along and sees him there and puts him in a car and drove him to the hospital and saved his life. But that's the only violent story I've heard of. I don't know anyone who has been shot . . . it's a strange atmosphere to live in. Talk about that. . . . Like there's a lot, yeah, okay . . . I guess in my neighborhood there's been a lot of purse-snatching. Probably done by little kids goin' after women at night.

M-32   Young Boy
Ruth Melberg, June 13, 1977

In Williamsburg, a young boy was coming out of the religious school. He belonged to the Chassidic sect of the Jews. He went into the telephone booth to make a phone call, and two boys went in after him, and they didn't even ask him for money. They just took out a knife and stabbed him. They stabbed him three times, and they ran away, and they said, "I got a Jew! I got a Jew!" They were hilarious about it, and this sixteen-year-old boy was killed for nothing.

M-33   English Professor
Marvin Woltz, November 26, 1977

I had an English teacher who used to live by Columbia, and he lost all our final papers because he got mugged and they took his suitcase from him. It was good, though, cause we didn't have to do them over. We just had to convince him how good the papers were! [laughs]

M-34   Lost Papers
Ruth Melberg, June 13, 1977

Ah, a couple of days ago, well, they threw her down and grabbed her purse, and then they just grabbed her purse. Thank God they didn't hurt her. The first time she was mugged she lost her whole bag. I don't know whether she lost money or not. She lost her glasses. But the papers are the most important thing. But it's a frightening experience.

M-35   The Parking Lot
Esther Ring, March 20, 1976

Why, in Building Seven a guy came in and whatchamacallit. Right in the back [of the building]! And he goes into the entrance, and he was mugged. Right on the spot! She ought to move out! [talking about a neighbor who lives in Building Seven]

M-36   So, That's Nothing
Ruth Melberg, March 21, 1976
See chapter 3.

M-37   The Classroom
Esther Ring, March 20, 1976

Well, while she [daughter] was in the classroom conducting classes, they came into the classroom, and in front of the class they beat her up and stole her bag. Mugged her!

M-38   A Third of the Blade
Steve Handelman, December 1, 1976
(Collected from New Yorker in Bloomington, Indiana.)

When I did get held up, a big black dude . . . he had a knife tucked inside his sleeve so when he opened his hand, in the palm of his hand lies the blade, only about a third of the blade of this knife. I just can't imagine how long this knife is. I mean, it was a straight blade running from the inside to his palm to his finger. I flipped. I swear. I almost popped out of my shorts. "Here, boom, take it easy!" I said to him.

M-39   The Bill
Tom Christiansen, March 25, 1978
See chapter 2.

M-40   The Soup Can
Marcia Bobson, November 10, 1976

I was walking crosstown on Fifty-seventh Street East, and I was right on 250 West Fifty-seventh Street. There were some guys taking stuff into a building, and it looked like a delivery. And these guys were real icky—and before I knew what was happening, he was molesting me. I had a little purse like a suitcase; not a shoulder bag. And it was a reflex, and I hauled it into him. Really hard, really hard. And he was crying. And he stepped back, and he was looking at me. And everybody was looking at me. Nobody intervened. And the guy yelled, first, he yelled, "Goddamn!" And then he yelled, "Fuck you!" All these people were looking. And I hauled again, and he ducked. And I yelled, "Get him! You should beat him up! He was feeling on me!" And these other guys were coming towards me, and I ran west to my apartment. My husband was there. I was upset. We were new in town. All the time I was in Chicago, nothing ever happened. I took a Campbell soup can in my purse so the next guy who got me would die. I was really ready. I carried it for over a year. It was probably chicken noodle or cream of mushroom. That made me walk aggressively. I felt very violent. I hated construction workers.

M-41   The Bicycle
Louise Stone, March 20, 1976

That's right. What happens? Either I'm carrying a pocketbook or they come up to you and snatch a pocketbook and keep on running. Some of them are on bicycles. So you're gonna run after them on a bicycle? You can't do it! There's so much crime in the city. And now with the shortage of police and firemen. Buildings burn, and they get to the buildings to put them out and lives are lost.

M-42   The Doorbell I
Clara Gold, March 23, 1976

E. W.: Do you remember the incident about Karen's friend Connie?
C. G.: Yeah, the beating on the staircase. Something about there's an airshaft in the building or something. I don't really remember. Something about they didn't get along too well with their neighbors. Someone rang the doorbell one day, or somebody had been harassing them by ringing the doorbell and running away. Her husband went to answer the doorbell one day. It happened a couple of times, and no one was there. There was no one there, and he went to answer it. And it rang a fourth and a fifth time. And there were two guys out there who just beat the ka-pock out of him. Apparently, he was messed up pretty badly. And Connie was hysterical because she thought, "My God, what if I had answered the door?" He was very close to being killed. It's incredible.

M-43   The Doorbell II
Karen Kent, March 27, 1976

It was Christmas time. They had a Christmas tree up. They had a lot of things there, like a new suede jacket and all sorts of presents underneath the tree. Jim came home from work. The apartment had been busted into. And their whole apartment had been turned upside down, inside out. It was all wrecked, and everything was gone . . . all the new things . . . new suede jacket. They went to the closet, and they [the burglars] took out stuff. And, ah, they way they got in was in the kitchen; there used to be a dumbwaiter system with a dumbwaiter running through the whole building. It had been stopped, but the shaft was still there. So I think there was a wall. There was some kind of board or something. And it was busted into. They came in that wall with a dumbwaiter shaft. And that's how they came in. I think they knocked their way through. You can't get into the dumbwaiter through the roof, and it's closed, and you can't scale up to the fifth floor into the dumbwaiter shaft. So it had to come across the dumbwaiter shaft, and there's another apartment and an opening into it . . . so it had to come through there. They called the police, and naturally the police took all the information. Then they wanted to have it fixed [the hole up the shaft]. What they wanted to do was to have bars so that nobody could come in through it. So they complained to the landlord, and he had bars put up across the opening. So the people across the hall figure, I guess they got insulted, because they, the neighbors, thought "us, us innocents" and felt they were being accused of the theft.

So shortly after the bars were put up, the bell rang one night when Connie and Jim were sitting having dinner. I think, but I don't know, but someone said, "Don't answer the door until you find out who it is." And the bell rang again and again. And Connie said to Jim, "Don't go to the door until you know who it is." Then the bell rang again. But he opened the door and yelled, "Who is it?" He yelled this through the downstairs bell. And then he went out of the door. All of a sudden, the door slammed, and about three or four guys beat up on him. And he was all black and blue. And he was hurt bad. Oh! They recognized the kids. The kids from next door didn't do it. Some of them lived in the building. When the kids ran away, they ran downstairs, and they knew which apartment they ran into. They called the police. And the kids' mother said, "Oh, no, they didn't do it. They've been home the whole time." But they knew who it was.

M-44   Getting Off the Bus
Clara Gold, March 23, 1976

An elderly man from my place was standing on the bus. I don't remember where he was going. It was a couple of nights ago. He was standing towards the back of the bus, and it was very, very crowded. He was being jostled. He was trying to get to the back door [of the bus]. And he was saying, "Excuse me, excuse me, excuse me . . . excuse me." No one would let him through. And he thought this was very peculiar. He finally got home and found that his wallet with his credit cards, Blue Cross, Blue Shield, his driver's license, and $150 worth of cash is missing. He had his pocket picked. It's the kind of thing . . . it's pretty prevalent in New York. But you get this incredible sense of frustration.

M-45   Coming Home
Norma Schultz, November 26, 1985

This happened to Ray Kerman. She was coming home from work, and she was entering her building when somebody jumped her from behind. It was a black man, and he tried to wrest her pocketbook away from her, but she resisted and she began to scream. People came out. She retained her purse. And he fled, but before he did, he knocked her down. She broke her nose, and she broke something in her side. She landed in the hospital for a while, and she's now in a cast of some kind. It was unfortunate. It happened right in her own building, where she thought she was safe. And that's in a good neighborhood. That's in the Bay Ridge area. That's all I know.

M-46   Grabbed
Mark Nathansen, June 22, 1977

I was about eight years old, and these other kids, they must have been about twelve or thirteen, came up and they mugged me. They grabbed me. They grabbed me and they started hitting me. I don't remember if they had a weapon or anything. There were about four of them; about four of them. So I kind of ducked out and ran to the corner drugstore, and I told the druggist what was going on. And there was a lady in there, and she goes outside. And one of the kids was her son. There was one of her sons; her son who was trying to mug me. And she beat the shit out of him.

M-47   Watching
Robert Ross, June 23, 1977
See chapter 2.

M-48   Give Him Cake
Maria Diaz, June 3, 1977
See chapter 4.

M-49   Shadow Watching
Kate Whitefield, June 17, 1977

I was walking home. It's funny what happens in different parts of the city when you least expect it. This happened while I was living on Charles Street, which is really a super-nice street in Greenwich Village. I had come to my office, and I was really well-dressed that day. I know some of the tactics that the young kids who are mugging play. They'll see a well-dressed woman and go up and hit her in the small of her back, hit her, just to make her off balance and make her arms fly out and her pocketbook drop. Again, it's this reaction that you'll let go of anything you are carrying. It was night. It was winter. It got dark very early. I heard footsteps behind me, which isn't so strange because there are kids in the area playing and skateboarding. But they stopped very short behind me. This made me perk up my ears. I pulled myself together some more. I looked at my shadow. I'm a big shadow watcher of my own, and I saw there was a shadow sort of hovering behind me going from side to side. Then I felt somebody going for my arms. Not really strongly. Not as if they're using all their strength. Because if you take somebody by surprise, you can really pin them. But it wasn't that way. And it seemed half in fun. I made a very swift jerking motion with my elbow, and it really turned out to be a young black kid. I really frightened him, because I missed his jaw by half an inch. I turned around and gave him a really dirty look. He took off down the street. But he grabbed my arm so weakly, I didn't feel it was serious. I felt it was more like a joke. It was really strange, because I realized that that area is predominantly white.

M-50   West Eleventh Street
Kate Whitefield, June 17, 1977

A friend of mine, a fellow actor, was mugged on West Eleventh Street right off Fifth Avenue. It's strange, because that's such a dynamite area. . . . He was walking along the street, and it was around three o'clock in the morning. He was just coming home from a party. He didn't realize it, but the guy, a young Hispanic dude, had a cane, a walking stick, and a knife. The guy was walking towards him. It looked that way to my friend, who then sidestepped to get out of his way. So the guy sorta blocked his path, flashed his knife, and hit him. You know, took his money and his watch. And then he said, "Keep going, shut up, and don't hassle me." So my friend did.

M-51   The Watch
Kate Whitefield, June 17, 1977
See chapter 4.

M-52   My First Crime Story
Patricia Edelman, July 22, 1977

I don't know if I have that many stories, so I'll tell you the ones that I know. My first crime story happened when I came to New York in 1975. The very first person who came to visit me at my apartment on 118th Street and Morningside Drive was looking for my name on the entranceway—the very first person who came to my apartment. And some guy came by Morningside Park and held a broken bottle up to her neck and took everything.

M-53 How about It, Dear?
Pamela Day, March 17, 1978

About a year ago, let's see, I was taking a course at Marymount. I got home between ten and ten-thirty. I take a Number Ten bus at Eighty-fifth Street and Columbus [Avenue]. So one night I was going home, and I was walking on Central Park West to my apartment on Eighty-sixth. And this guy was coming up the other way. And he sorta looked at me and gave me the old, "How about it, dear?" And I put on my old stone face and walked, dat, dat, dat, dat, dat [singsong tone]. Got to my outer door; got to put my key into the front door, and *this hand* comes and grabs mine. He had turned around and followed me home, and I didn't lock behind me. So I missed his little trick. So first, I just stood there in shock. And he said, "A little shy, are you?" And I said, "Oh my God! That's the way to the doorbells." And I said to him, "If you touch me, I'm gonna start ringing these doorbells!" So finally he wanted a little action [laughter]. So he went went away. I mean, I didn't call the police even though I shoulda. I didn't even tell my roommate, because I didn't want her to be afraid to go out on the streets.

M-54 The Library
Irene Whitefield, June 17, 1977

The library was a scene of triumph. Joining crime fighters anonymous here. I was just . . . naturally when you walk down the street you do this [demonstrates: holding purse close to upper torso]. You become a penguin with your pocketbook, as if someone would walk by and rip it off, and that's exactly what happened. This guy was on that side where the revolving doors are. I was going, and a woman was coming out behind me. He was a really tough-looking black dude. She was fiddling with all her books. And her purse was open, and I saw him put his hand in and take out her wallet. It was really loaded with money and stuff. But my sister had taught me one karate hold on the wrist. She was just fooling around and showing me this stuff. Without thinking, I just grabbed his hand and twisted it in the same way she had shown me. He just backed off because it hurt, and he dropped the wallet. I just started screaming, "You're a thief! You're a thief!" I couldn't get vulgar with him, you know. But I just started yelling very loudly.

And naturally a lot of people came, and I looked to see if there was a cop, and unfortunately there wasn't. He looked at me, "You want a punch in the nose?" However, I wasn't afraid, because I was worked up and very righteously indignant. I also knew I had five pounds of books in my bag, and if I had to make a move I could crack his skull or cripple him and he would sing soprano. So I wasn't worried. But afterwards, I was really shaken. Everybody said, "How can you do it?" "What if he pulled a knife on you?" But I just felt that in the middle of the day in a place like this [a library in mid-town Manhattan] where there were so many people, it wouldn't be bad. However, I would definitely think twice about it again.

M-55 The Subway Ride
Daniel Cohen, June 19, 1977
See chapter 4.

M-56 Professor Mugged
Marvin Woltz, November 26, 1977

It was night school; no, it was day school. As a matter of fact, they just walked in, robbed the professor and everyone else, and just walked out.

M-57   Bus Mugging
Marvin Woltz, November 26, 1977

It happens on the bus line in front of my house. They get on at one stop, rob everyone, and then get off the bus. I guess I've been lucky. I guess I would move. I would move. I would be scared.

M-58   The Schoolyard
Betty Gerber, June, 1977

A couple of times when the teachers are coming out of the building, let's say about eight o'clock in the morning, there have been a couple of muggings. Especially going on the days when we get paid and we're walking to our cars. We have to be very careful. They know when we get paid. Walking to your car you have to be very careful. They follow you to the car. . . . I don't really know the whole incident, because it didn't happen to me. My friend's check had been stolen on the way to her car . . . two of them. A couple of children have also been accosted. But not recently, because now we have security guards. Before the security guards, we had problems with men hanging about in the bathrooms. It's a little better now, but not much.

M-59   Revenge
Mark Nathansen, June 22, 1977

This happened to my friend. He came from a broken home. He lived with his father. His mother lived with another man in another part of the neighborhood. His father was robbed and knifed while my friend was in the service in the mid-sixties. His father was mugged by a Puerto Rican hoodlum. When he came back from the service, he still had connections in the neighborhood subculture. He went to see some of his tougher friends to find out who this person was, and he had both his arms broken. And my friend boasted about it.

M-60   Memory
Mark Nathansen, June 22, 1977

No one ever got to me. I was never run off in that neighborhood. I mean, things were constantly going on in that neighborhood, especially with junkies and with regular thieves. There was Mary's daughter, who was mugged behind the stairs and became a very disturbed person afterwards. A very disturbed person.

M-61   My Father
Jim Kenny, June 16, 1977

E. W.: What happened to your father?
J. K.: I think he's forty-nine [years old]. My father was out. It was about, I guess, two o'clock in the morning. He was coming home. And some guy just walked up behind him and stabbed him in the back.
E. W.: Did he say anything to him?

J. K.: Not a thing. And a woman was across the street, and she seen it and the guy ran. And that was it. And then when he was lying there, the woman screamed and called the police and an ambulance. Next thing my father knew, he woke up in the hospital.

M-62 Pocket Money
Rose Lefferts, June 13, 1977

He [the husband] went into the store, and he said where these two guys came from he didn't know. They must have followed him into the house. You understand me? And no sooner than he got on the landing on the steps, that's when they took his forty-five dollars off of him. He said to me, "Rose, I've never seen these two men . . . I don't know. They didn't say a thing. They came up behind me." They put his arms around him like so [demonstrates] and the other one came around, and then they took the money from his pocket.

M-63 Oh, Honey
Rose Lefferts, June 13, 1977

Oh, honey, there are so many things. But you see, not knowing people, you understand me . . . it makes them tell so many different stories in time. Take for instance, now. A man lived down my street. He lived down a block from my husband and me. My husband was coming home from the store. I said, "What took you so long?" He says, "As a matter of fact, I was talking to a fella that just got mugged." I says, "Yeah?" He says, "Yeah"—"oh, you've been gone a long time." He got talking with these two boys. That's why you have to be so careful. Because a woman on Avenue A where I worked told me that a well-dressed man walked up to a woman; she was coming from a bank, and a man walks over to her and asked her for a certain number. She sees him on the street trying to figure out what this number was, looking around, and then they went and got into a car! See, it just goes to show you that's why you have to be so careful who you talk to, 'cause people don't know. . . . They're famous for that today. . . . Asking you questions. Maybe it's nothing that they don't know, but they get a conversation going just to get your attention, something like that, in order to get what they want. Don't you have to be careful?

M-64 The Train
Susan Weiss, June 4, 1977

This happened two years ago. My friend was on the train. She was standing between the cars during the rush hour and was going home. She had a shoulder bag. And somebody punched her in the mouth or the jaw or someplace. He grabbed her face, and he slipped her pocketbook off her arm. Oh, so that's another technique. Feel terrible for laughing [laughs].

M-65 Identification
Ruth Melberg, June 13, 1977

In Coney Island, which is rampant with vandalism and muggings, and everything else, there are a couple of senior citizen houses. One day, a man came downstairs from his apartment. He was in his seventies, and he was pounced upon and severely beaten. He was so severely beaten that he was taken to the hospital, and he was in the hospital for about two or three months. He identified the boy that beat him. After he got out of the hospital, he was in his home in a wheelchair. But the fact that he identified the boy that beat him didn't mean a thing, because when he got better, which was a few months later, he was able to leave the wheelchair and walk out of the house, he came down, and this same boy, because he identified him, pounced on him again and beat him so badly that the man had a heart attack and died. And the boy ran away. And the police don't know who did it. They feel that maybe it was not the same boy, that maybe it was another boy, because they run in gangs, and if you identify any one boy, you are afraid that the other boys will come after you. You just are not safe anywhere these days.

M-66   Mugger Money
          Mary Simmons, June 9, 1977
          See chapter 2.

M-67   Protect the Child
          Maria Diaz, June 3, 1977
          See chapter 4.

M-68   Stabbing
          Susan Roberts, June 18, 1977
          See chapter 2.

M-69   Bingo
          Mary Simmons, January 9, 1981
          See chapter 5.

M-70   Walking Home from the Opera
          Clara Gold, January 11, 1981
          See chapter 2.

M-71   Greek Cross
          Clara Gold, January 11, 1981
          See chapter 2.

M-72   Taxi Ride
          Clara Gold, January 11, 1981
          See chapter 4.

M-73   Coming Home Ernie
          Clara Gold, January 11, 1981

There's a guy at my place of business. Ernie Brown. Black, very classy. Great sense of humor. One of the nicest people you'd ever want to meet. He's about twenty-six, twenty-seven. He lives in Bedford Stuyvesant with his folks and his younger sister.

He's coming home about one o'clock in the morning from being with his girlfriend. Home from a date, and there are these two guys waiting on his front stoop. And both pull out knives. They hustle him to his apartment. And they start to go through the place, and they see who else is there. He says, "Now, guys, take whatever you want. Now, I got my folks and my little sister inside. And if anything happens to them, one or another, I'll get ya." They took him inside the apartment. They tied him up and started to go through the apartment, at which point his younger sister, who is in her teens, I think she's about fifteen now, woke up. Walked into her brother's room while these guys were running around. I think they took a stereo or something. And she's rubbing her eyes. She's half asleep, and she's saying, "Ernie, is there anything the matter?"—"No, go back to sleep." And she turned around and walked back and went back to sleep. And the guys left, leaving him tied up. So it wasn't till morning that they realized what happened. And there's this kid who literally walked right into the middle of a holdup. God knows what could have happened! It took about six years off Ernie's life. They were all very lucky. He's still got people on the streets looking for them.

M-74 The Coat
Ruth Melberg, January 9, 1981

And now there's a new thing. You can't even wear a fur coat, because they take the fur coat off of you. If you're wearing a fur coat—real fur—you're in danger of having somebody come up to you saying, "Take off your coat." There was an incident in which a fourteen-year-old boy was killed for a sheepskin coat that he got for Christmas. It was in the paper just a coupla days ago. These boys had robbed him for a sheepskin coat that his mother had gotten him, and this was last winter. So this winter she bought him one for Christmas. And I think she paid about $140 for it. And he went out with friends, and the same two boys stopped him and told him to take off his coat. But this time he wouldn't. So he wouldn't. So they shot him. And they took his coat. And the boy died. He's dead because he wouldn't give up his coat.

M-75 Gold Chain I
Ruth Melberg, January 12, 1981

We had one woman who had all her jewelry snatched from around her neck. And she said it happened so fast, she said she didn't even know what happened to her until her neck hurt, you know, with the burn mark on it. And she saw somebody running. But she was in such a state of shock she couldn't even talk. And this is not an unusual case, because you get these purse snatchers who know how to open your purse and take wallets out.

M-75 Gold Chain II
Ruth Melberg, January 12, 1981

Of course, with the gold chains, you can't wear any jewelry. Even in this development that's supposed to be "safe," there have been incidents. So people are more or less careful. In the summer we have a little park outside of the building. One o'clock in the afternoon, one of the women decides she has enough sun, so she's going upstairs. She goes to the door, and as she goes to the door two young fellows come by. They followed her to the door, and they started yelling, "I'm coming up, Lucille!" So she thought they lived in the building. But as soon as she opened the door, and our door is locked with our own key, soon as she opened the back door they ripped off her necklaces and her rings. And they ran. And this is a common incident here. I haven't worn jewelry in the longest time.

M-76 **Gold Chain III**
Susan Roberts, December 31, 1980
See chapter 2.

M-77 **Gold Chain IV**
Norma Schultz, December 31, 1980
See chapter 4.

M-78 **Sheepskin Coat**
Susan Roberts, December 31, 1980

My friend Katy was walking along Park Slope a couple of weeks ago with her boyfriend. He was wearing a sheepskin jacket. And these kids, young kids, came up to him. They asked her boyfriend to take off his jacket. At first, he refused. They were young kids, and they drew a gun, and said, "TAKE OFF THE JACKET!" He took off the jacket and gave it to them. And they just left. They didn't hurt them or anything, but she sorta witnessed it. She was with him, and they were directing all this stuff towards the boyfriend. You know, take off the jacket. They pointed the gun at him. She freaked out. She was immobile. In shock. She couldn't scream. She couldn't do anything. She was just so scared.

M-79 **The Elevator**
Esther Silverman, November 29, 1985

See chapter 2 for the first portion of this narrative.
She had been mugging older women. I was the youngest woman she had mugged. She was pushing them into their apartments and mugging them and really beating them. One woman would have been dead, but she had been saved because she was wearing one of those big, heavy wigs. And, uhm, she must have had something with Jewish women, because she had been working this neighborhood, or maybe it was an easy neighborhood to work. I don't know. I don't know. She had been in prison for a year. The police told us afterwards. She was mugging people in Bensonhurst, but she wasn't beating them like she was beating the Jewish women. When she got out of prison, we don't know if she had something against Jewish women or if she became more vicious in prison after the year in prison.

Anyway, we all gave a very good description of her, and I described her outfit. And she was wearing a coat she had stolen from one of the other women, 'cause she got into their apartments. She would ring the bell and tell them she had a package for a neighbor. They would open up to take the package, and she would force her way in, beat them with a gun, and ransack the apartment. And she would really beat them so that they would lie there [and] they couldn't really do much. Anyhow, one woman was taken to the hospital. They wanted to take me, but I didn't go. I should have, maybe, just to have it on her record, but I didn't go.

Anyhow, they caught her a week later, she was still in the neighborhood. Still walking around and with the gun. They couldn't arrest her until they caught her in an act of violence or doing something. But they were following her. They would spot her, and they would follow her. I was her last victim, because after that they were following her. She went into a building, and as she was going in, she took the gun out of her pocketbook and put it in her pocket. When they saw that, they knew she didn't have a license for the gun. So, when they saw that, they grabbed her.

We had to go down to the station and identify her, and we did. They found some of her stuff that she was carrying, some of the stuff she had stolen. They wouldn't go into her apartment. Why they couldn't get a search warrant, I don't know. I wanted my eyeglasses. That's all I wanted. Like I said, I was very cold-blooded about it, as if it happened to somebody else.

M-80 The Same Mugger
Esther Silverman, November 29, 1985

Another victim of the same woman, I don't know where she lives. I may have heard. . . . But she was on the phone talking to her sister when the doorbell rang. She said to her sister, "Hold on a minute, I'll be right back." She went to the door, and the woman said that she had a package for a neighbor. And she let her in. She didn't beat her, she pushed her into the wardrobe. Or she hit her once or twice and pushed her into a closet and slammed the door. And her sister on the other end of the phone heard it. And she came running. By that time, the woman was gone. She had taken all her things.

M-81 The Train Station
Esther Silverman, November 29, 1985
See chapter 2.

M-82 Jogger
Esther Silverman, November 29, 1985
See chapter 2.

M-83 Hall Mugging
Bobbi Taylor, November 26, 1985

This was when I was living on the Lower East Side on Seventh Street between Avenues B and C. This was many years ago . . . probably around the late 1960s rather than the early 70s because of the context. . . . I was coming from Hunter College. I had just been having one of my marathon sessions with a professor . . . for my master's thesis. And I had a ton of books that I was carrying in my arms. Both arms. Those were the days when I didn't have a book bag. People didn't have book bags then. I had a little purse that was sort of of stuck down between my books and my bust. I had a dollar. That's all I had was a dollar. And so I got off the subway, and I took the Avenue B bus, and I got off at Avenue B between Seventh and Eighth streets. And it was late. It was like eleven, eleven-thirty at night. So, I'm walking to my house. We didn't have a lock on the front door. So I just pushed the door with my shoulder, which is what I always did. And I didn't have hands because I was carrying books. And there were two guys behind me, and they looked like friends of upstairs neighbors. So I held the door for them. Both doors, the outside door and the inside door. I held the door for them because I'm a polite person. Then I start trudging up the stairs with my armful of books and the one dollar in my purse stuck between my books and my bosom. And the next thing I know is that these guys are real close behind me, and I feel a hand over my mouth. And he starts to pull me. At first, I was angry. I opened the door for this motherfucker! I got real angry. He does this after I open the door for him! I thought, I only have a dollar. Let me give him the dollar. Then, no, I thought. He'll kill me. That's not enough for a fix. And so I could feel he was shorter than me 'cause he was reaching up. He had a hand up against my mouth. So I just let myself fall back. We went bouncing down a flight of stairs with him underneath me. He was a little shrimpy fellow. And his partner took off as soon as he saw us coming.

And he looked up at me. And then my old neighbor came out and started rattling garbage cans. He was really a crazy old guy. He always rattled the garbage cans. And this guy looked up at me, and then he hobbled away. So they didn't get my dollar. And I was able to get my vindication. And I won't leave New York.

M-84   Walking Home
Ellen Axelrod, November 29, 1985

I was walking. It must have been into winter, because it was about six-thirty or so, but it was already dark. And it was in the same neighborhood that I'm in now, but I lived about ten blocks over. It's sort of a lot of one- or two-family houses. I had to talk five blocks to the junior high school to the parents' association meeting. . . . So, I had to walk five blocks, but it was not a heavily traveled street. People in that neighborhood did not walk out at night. It wasn't a route to a bus or a train or anything. But I felt very safe there. And I was walking, and my mind was sort of wandering. I was thinking about something or other, and I noticed this car came around the corner awfully slow. I did notice it, but not enough to pay attention. So once it went out of sight—I think it actually crossed in front of me—but once it passed, as I said, I went back to thinking what I was thinking about. The next thing I know, this guy is walking very fast towards me, pretending he had some kind of weapon. And he says, "Give me all the money you got." He seemed kind of nervous. And I had already heard these kinds of stories, so I had already determined that I wasn't going to fight, and I would give him all my money. I wasn't even nervous at the time. Later it began to show. I said, "All right." He said, "I don't want to hurt you, just give me your money." I said I didn't think I have too much money. I didn't. He says, "Well, how much do you have?" I said, "Five dollars." And he waited while I fished around in my pocketbook for the money. So he didn't grab the bag, and he didn't grab the wallet. He waited until I fished out my money. So, I didn't lose my bag. Oh, and then he said, "Turn around, you know, and don't turn around." And then he left. So that car that had gone by slowly, he got into that car. The way that I look at it is they were riding around in the area looking for somebody alone, a target. And he was probably an apprentice.

M-85   January Evening
Ellen Axelrod, November 25, 1985
See chapter 4.

M-86   Canvassing
Ellen Auerbach, November 25, 1985

Well, I was with two other women, and we were going to an apartment building on a street with a lot of low-income folks to collect signatures to put an independent candidate on the ballot. . . . And we arrived in my friend's car, which was relatively new, a Toyota station wagon. And there was a guy sort of hanging around. But we didn't pay much attention [to him]. We managed to find a [parking] spot nearby, and we got out. And we went into the building. Before we could get into the lobby way, this guy comes in. [He shouts,] "Give me everything you got on you!" And he particularly bothered my friend who was driving. "Give me the keys to your car!" She had a dojigger besides the key, this round thing [Chapman lock], and in order to start the car you needed that thing. I think she handed him that thing. But he kept saying, "Give me the keys to your car!" And meanwhile, another woman had a ring on, and she got a little hysterical, the other woman. And he said, "Give me the ring!" Actually, he didn't even say "Give me the ring," because he was interested in the car, but this other woman got so nervous. She said, "Don't take the ring. It's the only thing I have from my mother." Sentimental value. And she went on and on. Well, he took the ring. I don't think I had any jewelry on. I just sort of stayed quiet and calm. And my other friend was also cool about it. Meanwhile, these two other guys are coming in, and we're just sitting there like dummies. And these two other guys go into the hall. And finally, he left. And he got very little except this woman's ring. Since we were going into the building to collect signatures, we didn't have a lot of money or pocketbooks or anything. And these two guys came out again. And the woman who had gotten hysterical and had in a way given away the ring started yelling at them: "Why didn't you do something?" They said, "We didn't know. Why didn't you tell us something was going on? Yell out, whatever." The woman who got hysterical just ran out of the building in hysteria. We had to go looking for her. She just went home on the train. She had like a paranoid reaction. "Why did it happen to me?" And there were three of us at the time! She must have been in a bad state at the time. She doesn't get quite that hysterical anymore. And that was the end of the petitioning. And that's the end of the story.

M-87   Christmas Mugging
Bobbi Taylor, November 29, 1985

This was around Christmas time, around '70 or '71. There was this guy I had always seen in the neighborhood. Big, tall, galumpfy fellow. He had huge feet. He had a huge dog. And he would always walk his dog in the park. He was sort of a shy fellow. And we would say, "Hi." Anyway, I was once again coming home late. And he comes up behind me, and he sticks something in my rib, and he says, "Give me your money" [weak tone]. And I say, "Get your finger out of my rib. I'm ticklish." And I said, "What are you doing? This is ridiculous. You can't do this. You can't bump the people off that you say hello to in the park." And I said, "Why are you doing this?" And he said, "I don't have any money to buy a Christmas present for my mother." I said, "You're going to get money by sticking up people with your finger?" I said, "Go home! You're going to get in trouble. Your mother will be happy to have you for Christmas. Go home!" So, he said, "Okay," and he went home. I continued to see him after in the neighborhood, and he never said anything, but he would always put his head down and look away whenever he saw me coming. He was just a sweet, gentle, little kid. Big and galumpfy. Those are my stories.

M-88   My Neighbor
Clara Gold, December 1, 1985
See chapter 2.

M-89   Visiting New York City
Barbara Fenwick, July 7, 1985
See chapter 5.

MR-1   Where's Ninth Avenue?
Clara Gold, March 17, 1978
See chapter 3.

MR-2 Murdered Mom
Debbie Rosario, November 17, 1976

Oh, like people would call me up when I was living away from New York. I had a girlfriend who called me up a couple of years ago. She was really upset. She was living in Queens with her husband, and it turned out that one of their friends, who also lived in Queens but in a different section, was murdered. A friend of hers was murdered. I didn't know the person. She went into this whole gory account. And she just had had a baby, her first baby. Her husband wasn't home. And she was alone with the baby. And someone just broke in and killed her with a broken-off bottle. Just slashed her to death with a broken-off bottle. . . . I don't remember all the details. She went into a lot of details about the bottle and how many slashes. And the baby was okay. He never bothered the baby or never found the baby. But they never found out who it was. The husband found her when he came home the next day. But she was really upset. That was the only bad crime I ever heard of.

MR-3 Next-Door Neighbor
Marvin Woltz, November 26, 1977

Yeah, we're the model city project. We had our murder about two years ago. It was a black kid. He lived next door to an old white guy. He had an argument with him ahd hit him over the head with a pipe. But the kid was legally insane and shouldn't have been out on the street anyway.

MR-4 Chassidic Woman I
Jill Polin, June 4, 1977

All I know is that she went to the East Side to buy a coat, and she never returned. They found her body in a trash can. I don't know if she was raped or sexually molested. They found that it was the super's son son who accosted her, raped, and killed her. He brought her down to the basement.

MR-5 Chassidic Woman II
Norma Schultz, Roberta Wolf, August 20, 1978
See chapter 2 for a discussion of this story.

R. W.: You heard about the Chassidic girl that got killed in this building? The girl was killed in the city. It was the worker's son—the elevator operator or something. Did you hear about that? The Chassidic girl—pregnant girl—who got crushed to death, or they found her in a garbage can or something.

N. S.: He tried to dismember her. She lived in the apartment above me. She was eight months pregnant.

E. W.: Where did it happen?

R. W.: It happened in the Garment Center.

N. S.: She had gone to New York to buy a coat for her mother.

R. W.: That's right.

N. S.: And she didn't return. And they went to New York. But she had not returned. It was during the week. And they couldn't find her. And they went looking around. Then finally somebody noticed there was a carton outside the building that was dripping blood. They opened it up, and they found a part of her. I went to see the husband. I went with a neighbor to pay my respects. It seems that she had gotten into the elevator. And the elevator has been slow, and she said to him, "Why don't you hurry up?" It was somebody she knew. And it seems that he was eating his lunch, and it seems that he was very annoyed and irritated by the bells ringing. He took her down to the basement, he raped her and sodomized her and stuffed her into the furnace.

R. W.: He must have not been well anyway.

N. S.: Well, of course not. And then he tried to dismember her. But they caught him, and then they had the trial, and half of the neighborhood was there. She had a tremendous funeral.

MR-6　Teacher's Wife
Mary Simmons, June 9, 1977
See chapter 3.

MR-7　New York City Lawyer
Daniel Cohen, July 19, 1977

A friend of mine who is a gentle lawyer, a nice, law-abiding, quiet, peaceful person . . . you would never imagine that he'd even had a gun. . . . There was a prowler who was looking in the house at his wife from the fire escape. Although they had gratings and it's practically unlikely that he would be able to do anything, nonetheless, he watched. One time, the prowler came though . . . came up through the side staircase. The wife called him [her husband]. He went to the dresser, took out his gun, and shot the man dead. Simply through the window . . . took out his gun and shot him. . . . Knowing that he was an East Side lawyer, and, oh, well, knowing that it was technically illegal. They said the man made a menacing gesture or whatever and there would be no way that my friend would be apprehended. And he had total equanimity, and he shot him. And the ambulance came, but he was already dead. He was a lawyer, a storefront lawyer. . . . But you know that people indeed did come in to hold him up. Although he never had a gun before, his excuse for getting it . . . the reason they gave him a license was that he kept it at home. It was just so odd—how matter-of-fact—I think that it was just flat out one more occurrence in his day.

MR-8　The Gang
Doris Connelly, June 16, 1977

This story is really vile. He had this friend who he hung out with . . . they're all really, really thugs . . . street gang. And this kid, I think he slept with this other kid's girlfriend. The kid shot him. The kid whose girlfriend was in on it SHOT the other kid. Killed him. At the funeral parlor, one night while it was closed, the other gang, the gang of the friend who shot the kid, really wanted revenge. So they broke into the casket, cut the guy's balls off, and shut the casket. Put them on top of the casket. Set fire to the place and left. That's the type of people they are.

MR-9　The Cousin
Bernadette Potter, June 16, 1977

This happened to a distant cousin of mine. This is *really weird*. They had just moved into a building, and the son was fifteen years old. He met these two guys who befriended him. You live in the neighborhood, so why not? Something like a month later, these two guys knocked on the door, and of course, the woman . . .

the mother . . . came in. . . . They ripped her off, tried to kill them, killed the mother. They took the son, slashed him several times, and hung him upside down in the closet for him to die. That's sick, yes?

MR-10 Professor Stabbed
Doris Connelly, June 16, 1977

There was a professor stabbed and killed on Amsterdam Avenue and 122d Street. Stabbed because a guy wanted his watch. It was a very precious gift. And he wouldn't give it to him. The kids stabbed him to death. That was about eight years ago. That was a very famous story. I believe that he was a philosophy professor.

MR-11 Just Delivered a Shot
Doris Connelly, June 16, 1977

There was a professor that was shot. You didn't know this? A dean was shot in his office by a former student at Columbia. Yeah, on 119th Street and Amsterdam Avenue. The guy had gotten out . . . he was one of those, like, black guys that got put on in the late sixties; did not do well, out on academic probation and was out and was very, very resentful. He came up several years later. This is the story I heard. This was before I went to school there. He came just right by the second floor, and the secretary tried to stop him. He pushed her out of the way. Went into the office and just delivered a shot. About six or seven years ago, '70 or '71 maybe.

MR-12 Lover's Return
Nancy Friedman, March 22, 1976

I had been dating this guy for about six months. Then I decided I had had enough of it . . . due to the socioeconomic differences and all that kind of stuff, we just weren't right for one another. And then it took about a month for him to finally realize that, "Hey, she means it." And we kept trying to patch it up and break it up and patch it up, and the whole thing didn't work. So anyway, it was Tuesday at work, during the day, and he called me, and I didn't call him back, and he called me a second time, and I still didn't call him back. I can't remember if I was really working or not. Anyway, he called, and I answered the phone. And he said, "Is Nancy Friedman there?" And I said, "No." And he said, "Do you know when she's coming in?" And I said, "I don't really know." He recognized my voice and asked why I lied to him. And I said I didn't have the time to hassle with him, and I didn't want to talk with him, and I don't want to keep hassling. "This is it. It's over." And he slammed the phone down. . . . And he said that he was going to strangle me if ever he saw me on the street. And I turned to one of my bosses who was in the office, and I laughed. And I said, "I just had my life threatened." And I must have been working, because I went back to work. When I finished working, I said, "Uhm, I have to go home. Five-block walk home from the subway." I kinda got scared. On my way home I was thinking I'd better change the locks, because he [the ex-boyfriend] had a key.

My cat always came to the door as soon as the door closed. My cat was always at the front door waiting for me. And when I put the key in the door, for some reason I dropped them, and I didn't hear Freddy's collar. And I got really scared. And I opened the door, and through the light in the doorway I could see that my couch had been moved. My couch had been moved. And I also saw there was no cat. And

I was absolutely frantic. I was petrified. The first thing I did was turn on every light in the apartment, screaming for Freddy. No Freddy. And that scared me more than anything else. The fact that my cat wasn't there. Ah, 'cause my boyfriend knew that one thing he could do to hurt me was to do something to my cat. Ah, I always told him, or he knew that the cat was the one thing outside of my family that I really loved.

So I'm screaming around for the cat, and I'm turning all the lights on. And I notice there was a hole in the wall above where the telephone was. So I assumed that he either put his fist or the telephone through the wall. And that's when he called me at work. He had already been at my apartment, which made me more uneasy. Still no Freddy, no crime, no nothing.

So then at this point, I was absolutely hysterical. I started banging my head against the wall and all kinds of crazy things. And there was one room that I hadn't looked in. It was a room off the kitchen that I had used as a little dinky room—it's really a one-bedroom apartment. It could have been used as a study, but I just did my ironing in there. And I walked in there and there laid my cat. And rigor mortis had already set in. And as crazy as I was before, I really went bananas. And I knew I couldn't call Mother, because she'd be asleep, which is a crazy thought to have in the middle of hysteria. But at that point I didn't know what was wrong. All I knew was that he [the cat] was dead. And then I called a friend in New York who I knew would be up. And all I did was scream. Well, somewhere before that I called the cops. I had called the police. And, ah, called her, and when she picked up the phone all I did was scream in her ear. I must have knocked out her eardrum or something. Anyway, she kept me on the phone, or I kept her on the phone, until the police arrived. It seemed like hours, but it was actually ten minutes. Then the cops came, and they were really nice. They seemed concerned, and they tried to calm me down, and we filled out all the information and stuff. But they couldn't take the cat away. I was going to press charges. They had to leave it in order that I could bring it to the vet to have an autopsy done, 'cause we couldn't figure out what had killed him. So the cops put me in a cab. They brought me over to my friend's in Manhattan. She took care of me that night.

The next day, April ninth, I came back home. One of the guys I worked with took me back to my apartment. We took the cat over to the vet's. The vet was really nice. I was still absolutely hysterical. They took no checks. So all I had was five dollars. They took my check. And then my mom picked me up, and she brought me back home for the next two days. I did nothing, and that was that. End of story.

MR-13 The Security Guard
Ruth Melberg, June 13, 1977
See chapter 3.

MR-14 The Subway Station I
Clara Gold, March 17, 1978
See chapter 1.

MR-14 The Subway Station II
Clara Gold, January 11, 1981

I don't remember which subway platform that was. Who the hell knows? Pick any subway in New York, BMT, IRT. It doesn't matter. She stepped on this woman's foot, and the woman looked at her and said something in words not more than four letters. And the woman said, "Gee, I'm really sorry, I apologize." And the woman said, "Well, just for that I'm going to push you in front of the train." So my friend, I don't remember which friend it was at this point, but I do remember the story, my friend just very calmly beat a hasty retreat, because there are so many nuts in New York you don't want to take a chance that this is the real McCoy. My friend went, "Oh, good!" and walked away from it quickly. That was the whole big deal. Obviously, she didn't push her in front of the train because she lived to tell the story.

MR-15 The Watchtower
Ron Ross, June 22, 1977

When I was at the Landmark Commission, I was assigned some work on the watchtower, which is the only surviving watchtower in the city. It's cast-iron, and it was built in the 1850s. It's in Mount Morris in the 120s. It's on top of Mount Morris Park. Of course, it's a high building. This fire watchtower is octagonal-shaped, and it had, I don't think it has it now, but it had a bell. . . . When I was working for them [the commission], it had a heavy cast-iron bell. Firemen would stand on top of the tower looking with binoculars out over the city. There were twelve towers at one point. This was the only surviving one. So I was assigned to work on it, because it was in pretty bad shape. I was trying to work on it, fixing it up. So I tried to get the Parks Department, 'cause it was in the city park, to send the money to fix it up. They said they couldn't do it for a number of reasons. One reason was they couldn't get heavy equipment up there, because there are no continuous ramps from the bottom of the park. There's just steps, no ramps. That's one of the reasons. Secondly, they said, "Well, another thing—crime." They said they can't get their workers to go up there. He's a worker and on their payroll, you know, and they can't order them to go up there because of crime. Because the workers are afraid. Now, it doesn't have to be one worker that would go up there. They could have five workmen doing the job. Apparently, even with five workmen they thought it would be worth it to say no. They didn't want to go up there.

Now, someone was killed one time when I went up there, with a lady who wrote a book on cast-iron architecture. And let's see, who was there? The park attendant of that park. So we went up there about two weeks before the murder. A guy with a camera was killed up there by someone. He was photographing, and two guys jumped him and stabbed him and stole his camera. Right near the watchtower. But I felt safe.

MR-16 Lovely Lady
Susan Roberts, December 31, 1980

Now that I'm thinking about it, a client who I knew very well in Brooklyn after I changed my job in the Bronx was raped and killed right on Ocean Avenue and Church [Avenue]. Oh, such a lovely lady. Her brother lived in her building for a year and as a client of mine, I only wanted to help her find an apartment for him. He was very frail. She didn't think he could take care of himself. So we finally found an apartment for him on Kings Highway. A year later she got raped and killed. Little lady, very frail herself. Maybe weighed ninety pounds. Quiet. She would do anything for anyone. And this guy followed her into her apartment. He tied her up. He raped and he killed her. He bashed her head in. It's a terrible story [near tears]. I liked her so much. You know what I think about when I think of her? How scared she must have been. Such a nice lady. That was in the news and in the papers. I worked with her for a long time . . . [pause, in tears].

MR-17 Antiques Dealer
Ruth Melberg, January 19, 1981

There was an incident here during the summer in Building Three. There was a man. He was a widower. He was in his seventies. He was an antiques dealer. Evidently his neighbors knew that his apartment was a very expensive apartment. How it happened I don't really know. But one day, the neighbors saw that his door was off its hinges. So when they went to investigate, they found the man bloodied on the floor, and he was completely robbed of all the antiques. The man was murdered for the antiques. They never found out who did it, and certainly it was more than one person, 'cause one person couldn't handle the door and the man at the same time. And this is something. You just have to keep quiet if you have any valuables. And you're very foolish if you keep valuables in the house, because in this day and age you just can't advertise what you've got. You don't wear what you have, and it's very unfortunate, because you wear jewelry out of sentimental value and certainly for pleasure. But what's the sense of buying jewelry if you can't wear it? Or what's the sense of buying beautiful things for your home if you can't enjoy them? Or if you invite people into your home to enjoy it with you? You're afraid to invite them in for fear of who's gonna tell the next one what you have. It's a very bad situation.

MR-18 Station Man's Son
Norma Schultz, November 25, 1986

This happened several months ago to the son of the man who owns the gas station where I buy gas. The young man picked up his friend, and they were going somewhere. This happened on Flatbush, on the corner of Cortelyou and Flatbush. They were about to make a turn, and this other car came by. And they were standing in line, but evidently the other car thought he cut them off. So, he pulled up on the side of him and shouted all sorts of obscenities. They didn't even answer him. The next thing he knew, he pulled out a gun and shot him and drove away. And he left the friend with a fellow who was dead, and he didn't even know it. They started to drive away. The car was moving forward, and they crashed into a tree. And then he realized he was dead. He died from a gunshot. That's it.

R-1 A Very Bad Experience
Kate Whitefield, June 17, 1977

A woman I met over the winter was down in Soho. She had a very bad experience. A guy tried to force his way into the apartment and tried to rape her. He didn't, but he did break her arm, which is really hairy. But how do you let somebody you don't know into your apartment? She was kind of shaken up. I didn't know her that well. I couldn't get all the details, but it was the sort of thing. . . . You know, it has been a problem. There's been a big batch of rapes in subway stations. And I have another girlfriend who's had a lot of problems at subway stops. I have a girlfriend who goes uptown a couple of mornings very early, like at seven-thirty, and one of them happened at her stop. One incident happened at our stop, at seven in the evening. This is when you imagine that things will be pretty cool. As soon as you hear something like that—people get tensed up, and I start to think that I should cancel my appointments, and you know, you really got to hustle to get home early.

R-2   **The Florist's Messenger**
         Susan Roberts, June 17, 1977

This man was following her home, you see. So she opened the door. He said he had roses. Someone had sent them from a florist. And she's looking for the card while he is standing in the hall, and there's no card. Anyway, he pushed his way in. He was this young guy, about nineteen years old. He pushed her in the bedroom with the two kids, and he took chains and chained both her arms to the bedpost. And the kids went hysterical, screaming, hysterical screaming. And, uh, he stripped her, ripped off all her clothes. The kids are crying hysterical. He locked the bedroom door. He started taking off his clothing. She kept appealing to him just in terms of the kids. And she was crying. "What are you doing to my children?" She was hysterical, "My children!" And finally he said, "I can't do this to your kids." And he dressed her, put her clothing back on, his clothing back on. He had candy, and he gave it to the kids. He said, "I'm sorry," and left. Meanwhile, the kids were five and seven, and they have been going to a psychiatrist ever since. They really flipped out.

R-3   **Wrong Place, Wrong Time**
         Doris Connelly, June 16, 1977
         See chapter 2 for a discussion of this story.

There's another one that was in the paper at Columbia. This sophomore girl— and I don't know how she did this, being a sophomore—took the Number Three train instead of the Number One. Instead of getting off at 96th [Street], changing for the local [subway] to get off at Columbia [University], she stayed on. She got off on 116th Street. The numbers are the same, I think: 103, 110, 116 [names subway stops in succession], except they're on Lexington Avenue. VERY BAD. It's on the other side of Morningside Park. She got out and realized her mistake. It was about five o'clock in the afternoon. She decided to walk through the park. On the way, she met this gang of boys, about five or six or them, aged ten to maybe eighteen. They all successively raped her. She got raped like a few times by that gang. Then she started to run after they were done and got stopped another time by this huge guy. He raped her. And then she ran the rest of the way home. She got raped like four times in the same afternoon. It was written up in the *Spectator* [the Columbia University student newspaper]. She was interviewed about a week later. She said it didn't bother her. She just realized what the situation was, and she was in the wrong. She wasn't traumatized by it at all. She said, "I was in the wrong place at the wrong time. I made a mistake, and this weird thing happened to me." She wasn't traumatized by it. Really weird.

R-4   **No Cash**
         Clara Gold, March 23, 1976
         See chapter 2.

R-5   **Don't Touch That Door**
         Bernadette Potter, July 16, 1977
         See Introduction for the beginning of this story.

I went like this [demonstrates] as he was going down the stairs, because I was still on the ground. My hands started to bleed profusely. I just put on my jacket, went down to the fourteenth floor, and just knocked on all the doors. People came out. They called the police. I stood there. I was afraid to go back upstairs. Afterwards, a couple of minutes passed, and the police came up and said, "It's all right to get dressed now." He took the blade. He took a handkerchief—just like you do in the police movie. So that . . . I don't remember where he took me first. I guess it was down to the police, to the project police, where they talk to you and stuff. I just don't remember. . . . So I wound up in the hospital, because I wound up cutting these two fingers so deeply. See, I still can't bend them [demonstrates]. The tendons were cut . . . but the thing is, I don't feel that bad about it. Because I knew that this person was sick. But he was eventually caught, because when I went like this [again demonstrates], I cut him on the back of his heel. I didn't know that then. So within five minutes, maybe fifteen minutes, he was caught. Positive identification, the whole bit. So that was kind of the end of that.

R-6   Laundry Room
Mary Simmons, June 9, 1977

I live in a nice area, a safe neighborhood. There's a rapist running around my neighborhood that the police know about and have witnesses against him, but he's still running around. . . . My girlfriend who lives two blocks away on Avenue X around the corner from me . . . she was in her laundry room at six o'clock in the evening—daytime—trying to get her laundry. She was getting ready to get into the elevator, and this so-called rapist pushed her into the elevator. He didn't rape her. She was lucky. They went up to the roof. This is wintertime. Now, it's bitter cold. He made her strip completely and started saying to her, "Suck me, blow me, I want you to suck me, blow me." She was saying, "Look, take it easy." She was talking to kill time, and they thought they heard somebody coming. He ran. Grabbed her panties and ran. He's a bastard. Grabbed her panties and ran. So she went home. She was jittery. She called the cops just like you're supposed to do. Reported it.

R-7   Do You Have the Time?
Mary Simmons, June 9, 1977
See chapter 4.

R-8   Ocean Parkway
Ellen Schwartz, July 20, 1977

When I was twelve years old, one of my schoolmates was gang-raped and beaten to a pulp. It was on Ocean Parkway. I won't mention any names. She's now a professional actress. But that was an isolated incident, and everyone was terribly shocked. But it wasn't as if it was happening all the time like now. When I think of the women that I know now who have been raped, it's like an epidemic—rape.

R-9   Four O'Clock in the Morning
Ellen Schwartz, July 20, 1977

Oh, then there is the thing that happened across the street from me. Last July, the end of July. It was almost a year ago, I think it was July twenty-third. And it was four-thirty in the morning, and I had been very edgy 'cause for three weeks in a row on the weekends I had seen this guy lurking around trying to get into the apartment of the woman across the street from me. He stands up on the garbage-pail holders and looks into her window. One time I called the precinct, and they never bothered to do anything about it. And then he walked away. Then one weekend I had no lock on my front door. This time I was a nervous wreck, because this guy was prowling around the neighborhood. . . . So it was four-thirty in the morning; I was back at my desk sitting at my typewriter, and I heard a scream. I went to the window, looked out of the window, up and down the street, and didn't see anything. Then I looked directly across the street from me, and I could see into the apartment directly across the street from me one flight down. We'll call it floor level. I could see the curtains were open and the lights were on, and I saw a guy beating the shit out of a woman. He was fully dressed, and she was in her nightgown. Then, honest to God, I couldn't believe my eyes! He zips down his fly and gets down on top of her and starts humping. And then I thought, I am witnessing a rape! I could not believe it! And I said to myself, "Hold on, now, you're too liberal; just because he is fully dressed and she is in her nightgown and he is beating the shit out of her doesn't mean that they don't know each other and they don't like it that way." I mean, you just can't scream rape at four o'clock in the morning in New York. So I had my police whistle in my hands, and I hung out the window and screamed, "Excuse me, is everything all right?" At which point he jumped off her, beat her up some more, raced to the window, jumped out the window onto the garbage-pail holder, and went running down the street. Whereupon I realized that of course he wasn't her friend. And I was hanging out my window blowing my whistle and screaming, "STOP, RAPIST!" There were a few people on the street who had just turned and stared. But I understand the precinct switchboard lit up like a Christmas tree. Needless to say, I telephoned the police and gave them the address of the woman. I called out to her from the window and asked her if she was all right, and she said, "Yes." And I called the police for her. I don't remember if I called 911 or the precinct.

I was really uptight. It took at least a half an hour for the cops to show up, where if they had moved their asses they could have tailed him and possibly caught him. I saw which way he ran. It's really unusual to catch a rapist in the act with a witness—unbelievable! But they didn't lift their asses to do nothing. . . . They came to see her, and they came across the street to see me. She came across the street in her nightgown and slippers to thank me. She was a mess. Her eyes were all bloody, she was bruised and battered. She said that he had his fingers down her throat and was choking the life out of her. She also said that he was holding a metal object to her throat. She thought it must have been a knife, but couldn't tell. She said that when he climbed in the window, he knocked over the flower pot, and that is what had woken her up and that is when I heard the initial scream. After that she didn't hear a thing because he had this thing to her throat. She sure was lucky. And she said that he was hostile. Obviously. But he said to her, "What's the matter, lady, afraid of getting pregnant?" Also she said that he couldn't get it up. I don't know if that is true or if she was just covering up. From my distance, I couldn't tell if he was on top or humping, but he did pull down his fly. I mean, she may have been protecting herself, or it might have been the truth. I've heard that sometimes in the case of rape this happened, that they sometimes can't get it up because of impotence. Sometimes, the women hide facts, too. Anyway, she said, "Thank you." And I said, "Put gates on your window, lady, 'cause I don't want to have to go through this again."

Anyway, I asked the cops if all this was confidential, and they said, "Yes, absolutely." And I told them everything that I saw: how this guy had been hanging around her the last few weeks on the weekends at four in the morning, and I reported him on two occasions. And on one of the two occasions I had reported it to the precinct. And they hadn't done anything to follow up. They could have prevented this whole thing if they had done a little legwork. They don't care.

R-10   Parking Lot
Ellen Schwartz, June 19, 1977

I was told yesterday by somebody that a woman was chased in a parking lot in Buffalo. And she went all the way home screaming, "Rapist." Nobody came out of their door. And this guy was chasing her around the parking lot taking off his pants!

R-11   An Embarrassing Situation
Susan Roberts, June 18, 1977
See chapter 2.

R-12   No Nails
Ellen Schwartz, July 19, 1977

I have a friend in the next apartment who was raped in October in her apartment on 101st Street. A guy climbed into the third floor. Eight feet isn't good enough anymore! It's got to be two flights up! He climbed in. She had nails to put in her window to lock it shut . . . but she forgot to put them in that night, and her boyfriend wasn't with her that night. This guy climbs in the window, and she was in a loft bed, and he woke her up, and he held a huge knife to her throat and raped her twice. He told her that he had been watching her and knew when her boyfriend was there and when he was away. He threatened that he was going to come back, and she screamed when she was initially raped. Her next-door neighbor was awake and was very uneasy. But she didn't do anything, and she didn't know what was going on. Then she [the victim] called her friend, and she never spent another day there or another night there. She left immediately, and her friends convinced her to report it to the police. She was in therapy at the time. She said she went through every conceivable emotion: anger, hatred, depression, you know, all the stuff. She seems to have come through it remarkably well; it's really amazing. I think I would have freaked out, even after witnessing the attempted rape that I witnessed. It had such an incredible impact on me that I left the city for six weeks.

R-13   Bad Vibrations
Mary Simmons, January 9, 1981

Yes, I remember that. I think it was in my building. I know who it was. It was my friend's wife. That's right. He lived on Avenue X right on the corner of Coney Island Avenue. She was in the laundry room. Thank God nothing happened! I remember the story now. She was getting into the elevator to come home or come back to her apartment. And this guy took her up to the roof. He wound up taking her underwear, if I remember correctly, and I think maybe someone started coming up to the roof or she was screaming. I don't remember exactly. She wasn't raped. She was shaken pretty badly, to say the least. She went flying back to the apartment to tell this guy she was living with. And I think he went up to the roof to see if anyone was around. Actually, the guy was gone with her underwear. Sick bastard. Yeah, I remember that. It was Renee.

Notes

INTRODUCTION: URBAN FOLKLORE AND THE NARRATIVES OF CRIME VICTIMS

1. All crime-victim narratives appear in their complete form in the Appendix, or in the text. See **R-5**.

2. See Appendix, MR-9. Bernadette Potter, interview with author, New York City, July 16, 1977.

3. Until recently, folklorists working in the urban environment usually concentrated on three groups: the transplanted ruralite, the visible ethnic, and the dissatisfied worker. Each approach targets a folk group within the urban setting, that is culture- or place-specific rather than urban-specific. These approaches are not always linked to the urban setting. See, for example, Richard M. Dorson, "Is There a Folk in the City?" in *The Urban Experience and Folk Tradition,* ed. Americo Paredes and Ellen J. Stekert (Austin: University of Texas Press, 1971), pp. 21–52; Ellen J. Stekert, "Focus for Conflict: Southern Mountain Medical Beliefs in Detroit," in ibid., pp. 95–127; Barbara Kirshenblatt-Gimblett, "Traditional Storytelling in the Toronto Jewish Community: A Study in Performance and Creativity in an Immigrant Culture" (diss., Indiana University, 1972); Bruce E. Nickerson, "Industrial Lore: A Study of an Urban Factory" (diss., Indiana University, 1976); Martin Laba, "Urban Folklore: A Behavioral Approach," *Western Folklore* 38 (1979): 158–169. The work of the Chicago School of Sociology has also played a role in the study of urban folklore. Sociologist Robert E. Park, in his benchmark essay on city life, claims that the city is "a state of mind, a body of customs and traditions." See his essay entitled "The City: Suggestions for the Investigation of Human Behavior in the Urban Environment," in *Reader in Urban Sociology,* ed. Paul K. Hatt and Albert J. Reiss, Jr. (Glencoe, Ill.: Free Press, 1951), pp. 2–32. For a "classic" article on urban traits, see Louis Wirth, "Urbanism as a Way of Life," *American Journal of Sociology* 44, no. 1 (July 1938): 1–24. See also Gerald Warshaver, "Urban Folklore," in *Handbook of American Folklore,* ed R. M. Dorson (Bloomington: Indiana University Press, 1983), pp. 162–171; an investigation of the applicability of Wirth's approach to studying the urban environment and its appropriateness to the study of urban folklore can be found in Barbara Kirshenblatt-Gimblett, "The Future of Folklore Studies in America: The Urban Frontier," *Folklore Forum* 16, no. 2 (1983): 179–234.

4. See Appendix, **M-28**.

5. See Appendix, **M-11**.

6. For a discussion of the various theories and methodologies that have evolved during the decades of folklore study, see Richard M. Dorson, ed., *Folklore and Folklife* (Chicago: University of Chicago Press, 1972); Jan Brunvand, *The Study of American Folklore* (New York: W. W. Norton and Co., 1978); Barre Toelken, *The Dynamics of Folklore* (Boston: Houghton Mifflin, 1979), esp. pp. 27–32. See also Dan Ben-Amos, "Toward a Definition of Folklore in Context," in *Toward New Perspectives in Folklore,* ed. Americo Paredes and Richard Bauman (Austin: University of Texas Press, 1972), pp. 3–15. For a succinct discussion of

the importance of studying folklore within a social/cultural context, see Richard Bauman, "The Field Study of Folklore in Context," in Dorson, *Handbook of American Folklore,* pp. 362–368.

7. For a discussion on folklore and the mass media, see Donald Allport Bird, "A Theory for Folklore in Mass Media: Traditional Patterns in the Mass Media," *Southern Folklore Quarterly* 40 (1976): 285–305; Ronald L. Baker, "The Influence of Mass Culture on Modern Legends," *Southern Folklore Quarterly* 40 (1976): 367–376; Roger E. Mitchell, "The Press, Rumor, and Legend Formation," *Midwestern Journal of Language and Folklore* 5 (1979): 5–61.

8. Roger D. Abrahams, "Personal Power and Social Restraint in the Definition of Folklore," in Paredes and Bauman, *Toward New Perspectives in Folklore,* pp. 16–30.

9. Aric Press with Jeff Copeland et al., "The Plague of Violent Crime," *Newsweek,* March 23, 1981, pp. 46–54. See also "Violent Crime Rose by 13% in 1980," *New York Times,* April 1, 1980, p. 16.

10. Mary Simmons, interview with author, Brooklyn, New York, January 9, 1981.

11. *Uniform Crime Reports: Criminal Victimization in the United States, 1977,* a National Crime Survey Report, NCJ 58725, no. SDNCS-N-12, December, 1979.

12. Stephen Schaefer, *The Victim and His Criminal: A Study of Functional Responsibility* (New York: Random House, 1968). See p. 60 for Schaefer's comments on crime statistics.

13. Louise Stone, interview with author, Brooklyn, New York, March 20, 1976.

14. Richard L. Madden, "Victims of Crime to Get State Aid," *New York Times,* August 2, 1966, p. 22; Ralph Blumenthal, "State Program to Aid Crime Victims Reaches Only a Few of Those Eligible," *New York Times,* March 15, 1973, pp. 45, 86.

15. Wirth, "Urbanism as a Way of Life," pp. 1–24.

16. Martin Gansberg, "37 Who Saw Murder Didn't Call the Police," *New York Times,* March 27, 1964, pp. 1, 38; Charles Mohr, "Apathy Is Puzzle in Queens Killing," *New York Times,* March 28, 1964, p. 21; "What Kind of People Are We?" *New York Times,* March 28, 1964, p. 18.

17. Paul Meskil and Robert Herbert, "44-Caliber Killer Shoots Two More," *Daily News,* August 1, 1977, pp. 1, 3; Joe Nicholson and Charles De La Fuente, "How the Cops Got Him," *New York Post,* August 11, 1977, p. 2; Charles J. Pelleck, "Caught! Son of Sam Is Captured," *New York Post,* August 11, 1977, pp. 1, 4. See also Mark E. Workman, "Son of Sam: As Interpreted by Crime Reports and as a Possible Source of Folklore," *Indiana Folklore* 11, no. 2 (1978): 151–160. Workman shows how journalistic reporting of the Son of Sam incidents affected the perceptions of New Yorkers, and how these perceptions changed with the capture of David Berkowitz.

18. Liddon R. Griffith, *Mugging: You Can Protect Yourself* (Englewood Cliffs, N.J.: Prentice-Hall, 1978); Charles Silberman, *Criminal Violence, Criminal Justice* (New York: Random House, 1978); Nicholas Pileggi, "Meet the Muggers," *New York* 14, no. 10 (March 9, 1981): 31–36. Both Griffith and Silberman address the point of the selection of victims by offenders. According to Griffith, p. 5, the "desperate" mugger does not select his victim but encounters him by chance. Silberman quotes a study on robbers and robbery conducted in northern California by Floyd Feeney and Adrienne Weir (*The Prevention and Control of Robbery* [Davis, Calif.: Center on Administration of Criminal Justice—Davis, 1973]), in which street robbers, muggers, and purse snatchers "seem incapable of . . . forthrightness and planning." Feeney's and Weir's research shows that more than

40 percent of the juvenile robbers whom they interviewed, and 25 percent of the adult offenders, had not even *intended* to rob anyone when they went out. 'It . . . was just a sudden thing,' one juvenile said. 'I didn't really mean to do it. I didn't plan it or nothing; it just happened. Just like that.' "

19. See Appendix, **MR-17**.

20. For a discussion on cognitive maps, see Peter Gould and Rodney White, *Mental Maps* (New York: Penguin, 1974), and Stanley Milgram, "The Experience of Living in Cities: A Psychological Analysis," in *Urban Man: The Psychology of Urban Survival,* ed. John Helmer and Neil A. Eddington (New York: Free Press, 1973), pp. 1–22.

21. See Appendix, **MR-16**.

22. See, for example, Susan Kalčik, " '. . . Like Ann's Gynecologist or the Time I Was Almost Raped': Personal Narratives in Women's Rap Groups," *Journal of American Folklore* 88 (1975): 3–11.

23. Susan Brownmiller, *Against Our Will: Men, Women, and Rape* (New York: Bantam, 1975).

24. See Appendix, **M-3**.

1. An Urban Storytelling Session

1. For a discussion on how social groups are used in the urban environment, see Morris Axelrod, "Urban Structure and Social Participation," *American Sociological Review* 21, no. 2 (February, 1958): 13–18.

2. Jan Harold Brunvand, *The Mexican Pet: More "New" Urban Legends and Some Old Favorites* (New York: W. W. Norton, 1986), pp. 114–115.

3. Leonard Feinberg, "The Secret of Humor," *Maledicta* 2 (1978): 89.

4. Gail Jefferson, "A Technique for Inviting Laughter and Its Subsequent Acceptance Declination," in *Everyday Language Studies in Ethnomethodology,* ed. George Psathas (New York: Irvington Publications, 1979), p. 93. Jefferson, who has studied the rules of laughter and how they are employed in conversation, says: "Laughter can be managed as a sequence in which the speaker of an utterance invites recipients to laugh and the recipient accepts his invitation."

5. Susan Kalčik, " '. . . Like Ann's Gynecologist or the Time I was Almost Raped': Personal Narratives in Women's Rap Groups," *Journal of American Folklore* 88, no. 347 (January–March, 1975): 3–11.

6. For an informative study on urban deviants, see James P. Spradley, *You Owe Yourself a Drunk: An Ethnology of Urban Nomads* (Boston: Little Brown and Co., 1970).

7. Richard M. Dorson, *Land of the Millrats* (Cambridge: Harvard University Press, 1981), pp. 220–221.

8. Deborah Tannen, "Talking New York: It's Not What You Say, It's the Way You Say It," *New York* 14, no. 3 (March 30, 1981): 30–33.

9. Ibid., p. 31.

2. The Traditional Components of the Crime-Victim Narrative

1. William Bascom, "Four Functions of Folklore," in *The Study of Folklore,* ed. Alan Dundes (Englewood Cliffs, N.J.: Prentice-Hall, 1965), pp. 279–298. Bascom notes that "more than simply serving to validate or justify institutions, beliefs and attitudes, some forms of folklore are important as means of applying

social pressure and exercising social controls." In some African cultures, a variety of folklore forms "may be used to express disapproval." In the crime-victim narratives, social disapproval is directed towards the anonymous offender.

2. For example, in the traditional folktale, it is almost assured that the villain will be punished. See V. Propp, *The Morphology of the Folktale* (Austin: University of Texas Press, 1968); Max Lüthi, *Once upon a Time: On the Nature of Fairy Tales* (Bloomington: Indiana University Press, 1976); and Jack Zipes, *Fairy Tales and the Art of Subversion* (New York: Wildman Press, 1983).

3. William Labov, "The Transformation of Experience in Narrative Syntax," in *Language in the Inner City: Studies in the Black English Vernacular* (Philadelphia: University of Pennsylvania Press, 1972), especially pp. 360–361.

4. For an introduction to the personal-experience narrative in American folklore, see Sandra K. D. Stahl, "Personal Experience Stories," in *Handbook of American Folklore,* ed. Richard M. Dorson (Bloomington: Indiana University Press, 1983), pp. 268–276; and Linda Dégh, " 'When I Was Six We Moved West . . .': The Theory of Personal Experience Narratives," *New York Folklore* 11, nos. 1–4 (1985): 99–108.

5. Barbara Kirshenblatt-Gimblett, "Culture Shock and Narrative Creativity," in *Folklore in the Modern World,* ed. Richard M. Dorson (The Hague: Mouton, 1978), pp. 109–124. In her discussion of personal narratives recorded from Jewish immigrants in Toronto, Kirshenblatt-Gimblett found a fluidity of form in her narrative collection; that is, personal-experience stories often took the form of jokes, and in turn jokes could appear as personal-experience narratives.

6. Many articles about occupational folklore have appeared over the past several years. For example, see Jack Santino, "Miles of Smiles and Years of Struggle: The Negotiation of Black Occupational Identity through Personal Experience Narrative," *Journal of American Folklore* 96 (1983): 393–412; Robert McCarl, *The District of Columbia Fire Fighters' Project* (Washington, D.C.: Smithsonian Institution Press, 1985).

7. Kirshenblatt-Gimblett, "Culture Shock and Narrative Creativity," p. 115. In discussing the categories of narratives among her informants, she notes that "there is generally a telltale sign that distinguishes different narrative types."

8. See Linda Dégh, "Folk Narrative," in *Folklore and Folklife,* ed. Richard M. Dorson (Bloomington: Indiana University Press, 1972), pp. 54–83.

9. Joel Best and Gerald T. Horiuchi, "The Razor Blade in the Apple: The Social Construction of Urban Legends," *Social Problems* 32, no. 5 (1983): 488–500. A fear of crime in general, and a particular fear focusing on the threat of an anonymous offender striking innocent people, figure strongly into urban legends, as shown by the above article on Halloween sadism.

10. Richard M. Dorson, *Land of the Millrats* (Cambridge: Harvard University Press, 1981), p. 214. In his thin chapter about crime in the Calumet Region of northwestern Indiana, Dorson writes: "Like the ghost stories of an older time, which conveyed a thrill of unease and disquiet and mystery, so crime-tales of today titillate potential victims who—if they have not already gone through the fright— may one day be surprised by an attacker at home, on the street, or in a parking lot."

11. Paul Radin, *The Trickster: A Study in North American Indian Mythology* (New York: Philosophical Library, 1956); Roger D. Abrahams, *Deep Down in the Jungle: Negro Narrative Folklore from the Streets of Philadelphia* (Chicago: Aldine, 1963).

12. There are many choices in the urban crime literature. See, for example, Hutchins Hapgood, *The Autobiography of a Thief* (New York: Fox, Duffield and

Co., 1903); Mary Owen Cameron, *The Booster and the Snitch* (New York: Free Press of Glencoe, 1964); Edward H. Smith, *Confessions of a Confidence Man: A Handbook for Suckers* (New York: Scientific American Publishing Co., 1923).

13. Richard M. Dorson, "Dialect Stories of the Upper Peninsula: A New Form of American Folklore," in *Folklore and Fakelore* (Cambridge: Harvard University Press, 1976), especially p. 224. In establishing the dialect story's derivation as folklore, Dorson notes that one of the generic characters is the immigrant bumpkin, unfamiliar with the customs and mores of his new environment. Like the dialect story, the crime-victim story depicts the character as inept in his surroundings.

14. See Liddon R. Griffith, *Mugging: You Can Protect Yourself* (Englewood Cliffs, N.J.: Prentice-Hall, 1978).

15. Susan Roberts, interview with author, New York City, June 18, 1977.

16. Marvin Woltz, interview with author, New York City, November 27, 1977.

17. Robert LeJeune and Nicolas Alex, "On Being Mugged: The Event and Its Aftermath," in *Urban Life and Culture* 2, no. 3 (1973): 259–287. In interviewing middle-class residents in New York City, the authors investigated how victims see muggings as "unexpected incidents." They write: "One explanation for the off-guard mental state that applies to most of the mugging incidents and to those of middle-class respondents in particular is that the would-be victims felt essentially positive sentiments towards the settings in which the mugging occurred" (p. 267).

18. G. Malcolm Laws, *Native American Balladry* (Philadelphia: American Folklore Society, 1964), pp. 18–20.

19. Ibid., pp. 146–174.

20. See Melvin J. Lerner, "All the World Loathes a Loser," *Psychology Today,* June, 1971, pp. 51–55, 66; Percy H. Tannenbaum and Eleanor P. Gaer, "Mood Change as a Function of Stress of Protagonist and Degree of Identification in a Film-Viewing Situation," *Journal of Personality and Social Psychology* 2, no. 14 (1965): 612–616.

21. Steven J. Zeitlin, Amy J. Kotkin, and Holly Cutting Baker, *A Celebration of American Family Folklore* (New York: Pantheon, 1982), especially pp. 83–90.

22. Bibb Latané and John M. Darley, *The Unresponsive Bystander: Why Doesn't He Help?* (New York: Appleton Century-Crofts, 1970), pp. 25–36.

23. Ibid., pp. 25–36.

24. There has been an increasing interest in the female offender. See Freda Adler, *Sisters in Crime: The Rise of the New Female Criminal* (New York: McGraw Hill, 1975); Ann Jones, *Women Who Kill* (New York: Holt, Rinehart and Winston, 1980); Janet L. Langlois, *Belle Gunness: The Lady Bluebeard* (Bloomington: Indiana University Press, 1985).

25. Charles E. Silberman, *Criminal Violence, Criminal Justice* (New York: Random House, 1978), especially pp. 48–86. In discussing juvenile offenders, Silberman writes: "In the past, juveniles who exploded in violence tended to feel considerable guilt or remorse afterwards; the new criminals have been so brutalized in their own upbringing that they seem incapable of viewing their victims as fellow human beings, or of realizing that they have killed another person."

26. See Jan Harold Brunvand, *The Study of American Folklore,* 2d ed. (New York: W. W. Norton, 1978), pp. 135–136.

27. Kirshenblatt-Gimblett, "Culture Shock and Narrative Creativity," p. 117.

28. Brunvand, *The Study of American Folklore,* pp. 135–136.

29. Bernadette Potter, interview with author, New York City, June 16, 1977.

30. Irene Whitefield, interview with author, New York City, June 17, 1977.

31. Gerald Warshaver, "Urban Folklore," in Dorson, *Handbook of American Folklore,* pp. 164–165.

32. Jan Harold Brunvand, *The Vanishing Hitchhiker: American Urban Legends and Their Meanings* (New York: Norton and Co., 1981), pp. 48–53.

33. While several legends are set in New York City, the setting has generally not been a characteristic theme for interpreting urban legends.

34. Katherine M. Briggs and Ruth L. Tongue, *Folktales of England* (Chicago: University of Chicago Press, 1965), pp. 101–102. Neil Simon's *The Prisoner of Second Avenue* was later turned into the popular film *The Out of Towners.*

35. Briggs and Tongue, *Folktales of England,* pp. 101–102.

36. Ibid., p. 102.

37. Jan Harold Brunvand, *The Choking Doberman and Other "New" Legends* (New York: Norton and Co., 1984), pp. 37–41; Jacqueline Simpson, "Rationalized Motifs in Urban Legends," *Folklore* 92 (1981): 203–207.

38. Lyn H. Lofland, *A World of Strangers: Order and Action in Urban Public Spaces* (New York: Basic Books, 1973), p. 9.

39. Brunvand, *The Choking Doberman,* pp. 34–35.

3. THE TRADITIONAL STYLE OF THE CRIME-VICTIM NARRATIVE

1. For an interesting review of literature dealing with crime and violence in American folklore, see James Inciardi, Alan A. Block, and Lyle A. Hallowell, *Historical Approaches to Crime Research: Strategies and Issues* (Beverly Hills: Sage Publications, 1977), pp. 31–56; Bruce A. Rosenberg, *The Code of the West* (Bloomington: Indiana University Press, 1982); Olive Woolley Burt, *American Murder Ballads and Their Stories* (New York: Oxford University Press, 1958).

2. Inciardi, Block, and Hallowell, *Historical Approaches to Crime Research.* See their chapter entitled "History, Folklore, and Crime," pp. 31–56.

3. See Jan Harold Brunvand, *The Choking Doberman and Other "New" Legends* (New York: Norton and Co., 1984), pp. 71–73, 150–153.

4. Roger Abrahams, "The Complex Relations of Simple Forms," in *Ethnic Genres,* ed. Dan Ben-Amos (Austin: University of Texas Press, 1981), p. 197.

5. The Afro-American toast is filled with references about violence, especially towards women. See Roger Abrahams, *Deep Down in the Jungle: Negro Narrative Folklore from the Streets of Philadelphia* (Chicago: Aldine, 1970); Bruce Jackson, *Get Your Ass in the Water and Swim Like Me* (Cambridge: Harvard University Press, 1974).

6. Max Lüthi, *Once upon a Time: On the Nature of Fairy Tales* (Bloomington: Indiana University Press, 1976), pp. 47–57.

7. Ellen Schwartz, interview with author, New York City, July 19, 1977.

8. Robert LeJeune and Nicolas Alex, "On Being Mugged: The Event and Its Aftermath," *Urban Life and Culture* 2, no. 3 (1973): 267–270.

9. Nicholas Pileggi, "Meet the Muggers," *New York* 14, no. 10 (March 8, 1981): 31–36.

10. William Labov, "The Transformation of Experience in Narrative Syntax," in *Language in the Inner City: Studies in the Black English Vernacular* (Philadelphia: University of Pennsylvania Press, 1972), pp. 354–396; Ilhan Basgoz, "Digression in Oral Narrative: A Case Study of Individual Remarks by Turkish Romance Tellers," *Journal of American Folklore* 99 (1986): 5–23; Robert Georges, "Do Narrators Really Digress? A Reconsideration of Audience Asides in Narrating," *Western Folklore* 40 (1983): 245–252.

11. Roger D. Abrahams and George Fosse, *Anglo-American Folksong Style and Culture* (Englewood Cliffs, N.J.: Prentice-Hall, 1968).

12. See, for example, Sandra K. D. Stahl, "Style in Written and Oral Narrative," *Folklore Preprint Series* 3, no. 1 (1975); Richard M. Dorson, "Oral Styles of American Folk Narrators," in *Folklore: Selected Essays* (Bloomington: Indiana University Press, 1972), pp. 104–110.

13. Michael Wolff, "Notes on the Behavior of Pedestrians," in *People in Places: The Sociology of the Familiar,* ed. Arnold Birenbaum and Edward Sagarin (New York: Praeger, 1973), pp. 35–48.

14. Richard M. Dorson, *Land of the Millrats* (Cambridge: Harvard University Press, 1981), pp. 213–231.

15. Ruth Melberg, interview with author, Brooklyn, New York, June 13, 1977.

16. Interview with Irene Whitefield, July 17, 1977.

17. Bernadette Potter, interview with author, New York City, June 16, 1977.

18. Anne B. Cohen, *Poor Pearl, Poor Girl! The Murdered-Girl Stereotype in Ballad and Newspaper,* Publication of the American Folklore Society Memoir Series, vol. 58 (Austin: University of Texas Press, 1973). Cohen's study of the famous murder case of Pearl Bryant, and how this case was reshaped in the folk and popular mind, has some relationship to this study. However, Cohen's work on this one particular event and how it was viewed over time is much different from working with a large corpus of narratives of one subject type. Individual crime-victim events, if not sensationalized, rarely seem to take on repeated versions; what my study tries to show is that structure, form, and style constitute the traditional qualities of the narrative text.

19. Clara Gold, interview with author, Brooklyn, New York, March 17, 1978.

20. Joe Feury, Andy Soltis, and Clyde Haberman, "3 Die in Midtown Gunfight," *New York Post,* October 18, 1973, pp. 1, 3. Additional corroborative material can be found in Frank Faso and Henry Lee, "Kills 2, Is Slain in 34th St. Madness," *Daily News,* October 19, 1973, pp, 2, 30.

21. William Slattery and Cy Egan, "Guard Accused of Hurling Boy to Death," *New York Post,* May 4, 1977, p. 15; see also Patrick Doyle and William Neudebauer, "Rabbi's Son Thrown to Death from Roof in Sheepshead Bay," *Daily News,* May 4, 1977, p. 3.

22. J. R. Rayfield, "What Is a Story?" *American Anthropologist* 74 (1972): 1085–1106.

4. The Functions of the Crime-Victim Narrative

1. Stanley Milgram, "The Experience of Living in Cities: A Psychological Analysis," in *Urbanman: The Psychology of Urban Survival,* ed. John Helmer and Neil A. Eddington (New York: Free Press, 1973), pp. 1–2; Georg Simmel, "The Metropolis and Mental Life," in *Classical Essays on the Culture of Cities,* ed. Richard Sennett (New York: Appleton Century-Crofts, 1969), pp. 46–60; Erving Goffman, *Relations in Public* (New York: Harper Colophon Books, 1971), especially pp. 28–61.

2. Michael Wolff, "Notes on the Behavior of Pedestrians," in *People in Places: The Sociology of the Familiar,* ed. Arnold Birenbaum and Edward Sagarin (New York: Praeger, 1973), pp. 35–48.

3. John A. Robinson, "Personal Narratives Reconsidered," *Journal of American Folklore* 94 (1981): 58–85.

4. Livia Polyani, "What's the Point?" *Semiotica* 25 (1979): 207–241. See also

Roger Abrahams, "Our Native Notions of Story," *New York Folklore* 11, nos. 1–4 (1985): 37–47.

5. Richard M. Dorson, *Land of the Millrats* (Cambridge: Harvard University Press, 1981), pp. 229–230.

6. Kevin Lynch, *The Image of the City* (Cambridge: MIT Press, 1960); Peter Gould and Rodney White, *Mental Maps* (New York: Penguin, 1974), pp. 15–49.

7. Gould and White, *Mental Maps*, p. 37.

8. Mary Simmons, interview with author, Brooklyn, New York, June 9, 1977.

9. Robert LeJeune and Nicolas Alex, "On Being Mugged: The Event and Its Aftermath," in *Urban Life and Culture* 2, no. 3(1973): 262–264.

10. Helen Benedict, *Recovery: How to Survive Sexual Assault for Women, Men, Teenagers, and Their Family and Friends* (New York: Doubleday, 1985).

11. Irene Whitefield, interview with author, New York City, June 17, 1977.

12. Ibid.

13. Marcia Bobson of New York City, interview with author, November 10, 1976.

14. Marvin Woltz, interview with author, New York City, November 26, 1977.

15. Ellen Schwartz, interview with author, New York City, July 19, 1977.

16. Lyn H. Lofland, *A World of Strangers: Order and Action in Urban Public Spaces* (New York: Basic Books, 1973), pp. 57–60, 84–87.

17. Ellen Schwartz, interview with author, New York City, July 19, 1977.

18. Susan Roberts, interview with author, Brooklyn, New York, December 31, 1981.

19. Bernadette Potter, interview with author, New York City, June 17, 1977.

20. Nicholas Pileggi, "Meet the Muggers," *New York* 14, no. 10 (1981): 31–36.

21. Morton Bard and Dawn Sangrey, *The Crime Victim's Book* (New York: Basic Books, 1979), p. 15.

22. Linda Dégh, " 'When I Was Six We Moved West . . .': The Theory of Personal Experience Narrative," *New York Folklore* 11, nos. 1–4 (1985): 104.

23. Elisabeth Kübler-Ross, *On Death and Dying* (New York: Macmillan, 1969).

24. Martin Symonds, "Victims of Violence: Psychological Effects and Aftermath," *American Journal of Psychoanalysis* 35 (Spring, 1975): 19–26.

25. Leslie Bennetts, "Woody Allen's Selective Vision of New York," *New York Times*, March 7, 1986, p. C28.

26. Rose Laub Coser, "Some Social Functions of Laughter," *Human Relations* 12, no. 2 (1959): 171–182.

27. Norman Cousins, *Anatomy of an Illness* (New York: W. W. Norton, 1979).

5. World View and the Crime-Victim Narrative

1. See, for example, Herbert Ausbury, *The Gangs of New York* (New York: Knopf, 1928); Benjamin Botkin, *New York City Folklore* (New York: Random House, 1956); Bayard Still, "The Personality of New York City," *New York Folklore Quarterly* 14, no. 2 (1958): 83–92; Edward Van Every, *The Sins of New York As Exposed by the Police Gazette* (New York: Gale Research Co., 1976).

2. Pauline Kael, *Taking It All In* (New York: Holt, Rinehart and Winston, 1984), pp. 151–153.

3. Jan Harold Brunvand, *The Choking Doberman and Other "New" Legends* (New York: Norton and Co., 1984), Jan Harold Brunvand, *The Mexican Pet: More "New" Urban Legends and Some Old Favorites* (New York: W. W. Norton, 1986), p. 45.

4. Patricia A. Turner, "Jacksonalia: A Study of Contemporary Black Folk Heroes," presented at the Annual Meeting of the American Folklore Society, 1985.

5. James Gleick, "Survival: The New York Joke," *New York Times,* April 28, 1985, pp. 49, 66, 68, 70.

6. Murray Weiss and Dan Singleton, "Fear Spawns Subway 'Hero'?: Prey Turns Predator," *Daily News,* December 30, 1984, p. 5; Brian Kates, "A Fantasy Comes True: Death Wish Gunman Captured City's Imagination," *Daily News,* January 1, 1985, p. 2.

7. Tony Burton, "City 'out of Control': New Hampshire Bookseller Recalls Goetz Visit," *Daily News,* January 3, 1985, p. 30; Don Gentile and Brian Kates, " 'A Little Strange': Neighbors Describe Him as a Zealot," *Daily News,* January 1, 1985, p. 3; Myra Freidman and Michael Daly, "My Neighbor Bernie Goetz," *New York,* February 18, 1985, pp. 1, 34–41.

8. Willard Gaylin, M.D., *The Rage Within: Anger in Modern Life* (New York: Simon and Schuster, 1984), p. 47.

9. Leslie T. Sharpe, interview with author, December 29, 1984, New York City.

10. C. R. Creekmore, "Cities Won't Drive You Crazy," *Psychology Today* 19, no. 1 (January, 1985): 46–53.

11. Bronislaw Malinowski, *Argonauts of the Western Pacific* (London: Routledge and Kegan Paul, 1922), p. 517. See also Clifford Geertz, "Ethos, World-View, and the Analysis of Sacred Symbols," in *Every Man His Way: Readings in Cultural Anthropology,* ed. Alan Dundes (Englewood Cliffs, N.J.: Prentice-Hall, 1968), pp. 303–314; Alan Dundes, "Folk Ideas as Units of World Views," *Journal of American Folklore* 84 (1971): 93–103.

12. Gerald Handel, "Visiting New York," in *The Apple Sliced: Sociological Studies of New York City,* ed. Vernon Boggs, Gerald Handel, and Sylvia F. Fava (Massachusetts: Bergin and Garvey, 1983), p. 303.

13. Charles E. Silberman, *Criminal Violence, Criminal Justice* (New York: Random House, 1978), p. 63.

14. Richard Sennett, *The Uses of Disorder: Personal Identity and City Life* (New York: Vintage Books, 1970), p. 20.

15. Ibid.

16. Irene Whitefield, interview with author, New York City, June 17, 1977.

17. Patricia Edelman, interview with author, New York City, July 22, 1977.

18. Josephine Perrigo, interview with author, New York City, June 5, 1977.

19. There are many sources for trickster tales. See, for example, Roger Abrahams, *Positively Black* (Englewood Cliffs, N.J.: Prentice Hall, 1970); Richard M. Dorson, *American Negro Folktales* (Greenwich, Conn.: Fawcett Publications, 1967).

20. Lawrence Levine, *Black Culture, Black Consciousness* (New York: Oxford University Press, 1977), pp. 121–133.

21. Melvin J. Lerner and Dale T. Miller, "Just World Research and the Attribution Process: Looking Back and Ahead," *Psychological Bulletin* 85, no. 5 (1978): 1030–1031.

22. Roger Abrahams, "Our Native Notions of Story," *New York Folklore* 11, nos. 1–4 (1985): 39.

Selected Bibliography

Aarne, Antti, and Stith Thompson. *The Types of the Folktale*. Folklore Fellows Communication no. 184. Helsinki: Suomalainen Tiedeakatemi Scientiarum Fennica, 1964.

Abrahams, Roger D. "The Complex Relations of Simple Forms." *Genre* 2 (1969): 104–28.

———. *Deep Down in the Jungle: Negro Narrative Folklore from the Streets of Philadelphia*. Chicago: Aldine, 1970.

———. "Our Native Notions of Story." *New York Folklore* 11, nos. 1–4 (1985): 37–47.

———. "Personal Power and Social Restraint in the Definition of Folklore." In *Toward New Perspectives,* edited by Américo Paredes and Richard Bauman. Austin: University of Texas Press, 1972.

———. "Some Varieties of Heroes in America." *Journal of the Folklore Institute* 3 (1966): 341–362.

Axelrod, Morris. "Urban Structure and Social Participation." *American Sociological Review* 21, no. 1 (February, 1956): 13–18.

Babcock, Barbara A. "The Story in the Story: Metanarration in Folk Narrative." In *Verbal Art as Performance,* edited by Richard Bauman. Rowley, Mass: Newbury House Publications, 1977.

Ball, Richard A. "The Victimological Cycle." *Victimology* 1, no. 13 (Fall, 1976): 379–395.

Bard, Morton, and Dawn Sangrey. *The Crime Victim's Book*. New York: Basic Books, 1979.

Barkas, J. L. *Victims*. New York: Charles Scribner's Sons, 1978.

Basgoz, Ilhan. "Digression in Narrative: A Case Study of Individual Remarks by Turkish Romance Tellers." *Journal of American Folklore* 99 (1986): 5–23.

Baughman, Ernest. *Type and Motif Index of the Folktales of England and North America*. Indiana University Folklore Series no. 20. The Hague: Mouton, 1966.

Ben-Amos, Dan. "Toward a Definition of Folklore in Context." In *Toward New Perspectives in Folklore,* edited by Americo Paredes and Richard Bauman. Austin: University of Texas Press, 1972.

Benedict, Helen. *Recovery: How to Survive Sexual Assault for Women, Men, Teenagers, and Their Family and Friends*. New York: Doubleday, 1985.

Best, Joel, and Gerald T. Horiuchi. "The Razor Blade in the Apple: The Social Construction of Urban Legends." *Social Problems* 32, no. 5 (June 1985): 488–500.

Brownmiller, Susan. *Against Our Will: Men, Women, and Rape*. New York: Bantam, 1975.

Brunvand, Jan H. *The Choking Doberman and Other "New" Urban Legends*. New York: Norton and Co., 1984.

———. *The Study of American Folklore*. 3d ed. New York: W. W. Norton and Co., 1986.

————. *The Vanishing Hitchhiker: American Urban Legends and Their Meaning.* New York: Norton and Co., 1981.

Cameron, Mary Owen. *The Booster and the Snitch: Department Store Shoplifting.* New York: Free Press of Glencoe, 1964.

Coates, Dan; Camille B. Wortman; and Antonia Abbey. "Reactions to Victims." In *New Approaches to Social Problems,* edited by Irene Hanson Frieze, Daniel Bar-Tel, and John S. Carroll. San Francisco: Jossey-Bass Publishers, 1979.

Cohen, Anne B. *Poor Pearl, Poor Girl! The Murdered-Girl Stereotype in Ballad and Newspaper.* Publication of the American Folklore Society Memoir Series, vol. 58. Austin: University of Texas, 1973.

Coser, Rose Laub. "Some Social Functions of Laughter." *Human Relations* 12, no. 2 (1959): 171–182.

Cothran, Kay L. "Talking Trash in the Okefenokee Swamp Rim, Georgia." In *Readings in American Folklore,* edited by Jan H. Brunvand. New York: W. W. Norton, 1979.

Dégh, Linda. "The 'Belief Legend' in Modern Society: Form, Function, and Relationship to Other Genres." In *American Folk Legend: A Symposium,* edited by Wayland Hand. Berkeley: University of California Press, 1971.

————. "Folk Narrative." In *Folklore and Folklife: An Introduction,* edited by Richard Dorson. Chicago: University of Chicago Press, 1972.

————. *Folktales and Society: Storytelling in a Hungarian Peasant Community.* Bloomington: Indiana University Press, 1969.

Dobos, Ilona. "True Stories." In *Studies in East European Folk Narrative,* edited by Linda Dégh. American Folklore Society Bibliographic and Special Series no. 30, 1978.

Dorson, Richard M. *Folklore and Folklife.* Chicago: University of Chicago Press, 1972.

————. "Is There a Folk in the City?" In *The Urban Experience and Folk Tradition,* edited by Américo Paredes and Ellen J. Stekert. Austin: University of Texas Press, 1971.

————. *Land of the Millrats.* Cambridge: Harvard University Press, 1981.

————. "Oral Tradition and Written History: The Case for the United States." In *American Folklore and the Historian,* edited by Richard M. Dorson. Chicago: University of Chicago Press, 1971.

Dundes, Alan. "The Devolutionary Premise in Folklore Theory." In *Analytic Essays in Folklore,* edited by Alan Dundes. Berkeley: University of California Press, 1975.

————. "Folk Ideas as Units of World View." *Journal of American Folklore* 84 (1971): 93–103.

————, and Carl R. Pagter. *Urban Folklore from the Paperwork Empire.* Austin: American Folklore Society, 1975.

Ellis, Bill. "De Legendis Urbis: Modern Legends in Ancient Rome." *Journal of American Folklore* 96 (1983): 200–208.

Feinberg, Leonard. "The Secret of Humor." *Maledicta* 2 (1978): 86–110.

Foster, George M., and Robert V. Kemper. *Anthropologists in Cities.* Boston: Little Brown and Co., 1974.

Freilich, Morris. *Marginal Natives: Anthropologists at Work.* New York: Harper and Row, 1970.

Freud, Sigmund. *Jokes and Their Relationship to the Unconscious.* New York: W. W. Norton, 1963.

Georges, Robert A. "Do Narrators Really Disgress? A Reconsideration of Audience Asides in Narrating." *Western Folklore* 40 (1983): 245–252.

———, and Michael O. Jones. *People Studying People: The Human Element in Fieldwork*. Berkeley: University of California Press, 1980.

Goffman, Erving. *Relations in Public*. New York: Harper Colophon Books, 1971.

Handel, Gerald. "Visiting New York." In *The Apple Sliced: Sociological Studies of New York City,* edited by Vernon Boggs, Gerald Handel, Sylvia F. Fava. Massachusetts: Bergin and Garvey Publishers, 1984.

Hunt, Morton. *The Mugging*. New York: Atheneum, 1962.

Inciardi, James A.; Alan A. Block; and Lyle A. Hallowell. *Historical Approaches to Crime Research: Strategies and Issues*. Beverly Hills: Sage Publications, 1977.

Jackson, Bruce. *In the Life*. New York: Macmillan and Co., 1972.

Jacobs, Jane. *The Death and Life of Great American Cities*. New York: Random House, 1961.

Jansen, William Hugh. "The Esoteric-Exoteric Factor in Folklore. In *The Study of Folklore,* edited by Alan Dundes. Englewood Cliffs, N.J.: Prentice-Hall, 1965.

Jefferson, Gail. "A Technique for Inviting Laughter and Its Subsequent Acceptance Declination." In *Everyday Language Studies in Ethnomethodology,* edited by George Psathas. New York: Irvington Publishers, 1979.

Kalčik, Susan. " '. . . Like Ann's Gynecologist or the Time I Was Almost Raped': Personal Narratives in Women's Rap Groups." *Journal of American Folklore* 88 no. 347 (1975): 3–11.

Karp, David; Gregory P. Stone; and William C. Yoels. *Being Urban: A Social Psychological View of City Life*. Lexington, Mass.: D. C. Heath and Co., 1977.

Kirshenblatt-Gimblett, Barbara. "Culture Shock and Narrative Creativity." In *Folklore in the Modern World,* edited by Richard M. Dorson. The Hague: Mouton, 1978.

———. "The Future of Folklore Studies in America: The Urban Frontier." *Folklore Forum* 16, no. 2 (1983): 175–234.

Klapp, Orrin. "American Villain Types." *American Sociological Review* 21 (1956): 377–340.

Klausher, Lawrence D. *Son of Sam*. New York: McGraw Hill, 1981.

McCarl, Robert. *The District of Columbia Fire Fighters' Project: A Case Study in Occupational Folklore*. Washington, D.C.: Smithsonian Institution Press, 1985.

Malinowski, Bronislaw. *Argonauts of the Western Pacific*. London: Routledge and Kegan Paul, 1922.

Mendelsohn, Benjamin. "Victimology and Contemporary Society's Trends." *Victimology* 1, no. 1 (Spring, 1976): 8–28.

Milgram, Stanley. "The Experience of Living in Cities: A Psychological Analysis." In *Urbanman: The Psychology of Urban Survival,* edited by John Helmer and Neil A. Eddington. New York: Free Press, 1973.

Nettler, Gwynn. *Explaining Crime*. 2d ed. New York: McGraw Hill, 1978.

Oring, Elliott. "Everything Is a Shade of Elephant: An Alternative to a Psychoanalysis of Humor." *New York Folklore* 1 (1975).

———. "Hey, You've Got No Character: Chizbat Humor and the Boundaries of Israeli Identity." *Journal of American Folklore* 86 (1973): 358-366.

Park, Robert Ezra. *Human Communities: The City and Human Ecology*. New York: Free Press, 1952.

Pileggi, Nicholas. "Meet the Muggers." *New York* 14, no. 10 (March 9, 1981): 31–36.

"The Plague of Violent Crime." *Newsweek,* March 23, 1981, pp. 46–54.

Polyani, Livia. "What's the Point?" *Semiotica* 25 (1979): 207–241.

Rayfield, J. R. "What Is a Story?" *American Anthropologist* 74 (1972): 1085–1106.

Robinson, John A. "Personal Narratives Reconsidered." *Journal of American Folklore* 94 (1981): 58–85.

Rosnow, Ralph L., and Gary Alan Fine. *Rumor and Gossip: The Social Psychology of Hearsay.* New York: Elsevier, 1976.

Schaefer, Stephen. *The Victim and His Criminal: A Study in Functional Responsibility.* New York: Random House, 1968.

Sennett, Richard. *The Uses of Disorder: Personal Identity and City Life.* New York: Vintage Books, 1970.

Shaver, Kelly G. "Defensive Attribution: Effects of Severity and Relevance on the Responsibility Assigned for an Accident." *Journal of Personality and Social Psychology* 14 (1970): 101–113.

Silberman, Charles E. *Criminal Violence, Criminal Justice.* New York: Random House, 1978.

Spradley, James. *You Owe Yourself a Drunk: An Ethnography of Urban Nomads.* Boston: Little Brown and Co., 1970.

Stahl, Sandra D. K. "The Oral Personal Narrative in Its Generic Context." *Fabula* 18 (1977): 18–39.

Still, Bayard. "The Personality of New York City." *New York Folklore Quarterly* 14, no. 2 (Summer, 1958): 83–92.

Tannen, Deborah. "Conversational Style." Paper presented at Conference on Psycholinguistic Models of Production: An Interdisciplinary Workshop. University of Kassel, West Germany, July 13–17, 1980.

———. "Talking New York: It's Not What You Say, It's the Way You Say It." *New York* 14, no. 13 (March 30, 1981): 30–33.

Tannenbaum, Percy, and Eleanor P. Gaer. "Mood Changes as a Function of Stress of Protagonist and Degree of Identification in a Film-Viewing Situation." *Journal of Personality and Social Psychology* 2, no. 4 (1965): 612–616.

Thompson, Stith. *Motif-Index of Folk Literature.* 6 vols. Bloomington: Indiana University Press, 1966.

Toelken, Barre. *The Dynamics of Folklore.* Boston: Houghton Mifflin, 1979.

———. "Folklore, Worldview, and Communication." in *Folklore, Performance, and Communication,* edited by Dan Ben-Amos and Kenneth S. Goldstein. The Hague: Mouton, 1975.

Tuan, Yi-Fu. *Landscapes of Fear.* Minneapolis: University of Minnesota Press, 1979.

———. *Topophilia: A Study of Environmental Perception, Attitudes and Values.* Englewood Cliffs, N.J.: Prentice-Hall, 1974.

Uniform Crime Reports: Criminal Victimization in the United States, 1977. A National Crime Survey Report, NCJ58725, no. SDNCS-N-12, December, 1979.

Viano, Emilo C. "Victimology: The Study of the Victim." *Victimology* 1, no. 1 (Spring, 1976): 1–7.

Wachs, Eleanor. "The Crime-Victim Narrative as a Folkloric Genre." *Journal of the Folklore Institute* 19, no. 1 (1982): 17–30.

Watson, Jeanne, and Robert J. Potter. "An Analytic Unit for the Study of Interaction." *Human Relations* 15 (1962): 245–263.

Wirth, Louis. "Urbanism as a Way of Life." *American Journal of Sociology* 44, no. 1 (July, 1938): 1–24.

Wohl, R. Richard, and Anselm L. Strauss. "Symbolic Representation and the Urban Milieu." *American Journal of Sociology* 63 (March, 1958): 523–32.

Index

Allen, Woody: humor and anxiety, 74. *See also* Comedians; Humor

Apathy: urban frustration, 4; narrative category of crime-victim story, 25–26; bystander in crime-victim story, 44–45

Audience: role in crime-victim narration, 2

Auerbach, Ellen: mugging account, 110–11

Axelrod, Ellen: mugging accounts, 70, 110

Bobson, Marcia: mugging account, 42, 99

Bower, Joe: mugging account, 48, 95

"The Central Park Jogger": urban legend as crime-victim story, 35–36; suspicion as message, 37

Characters: general feature of crime-victim story, 17–18; lack of development in crime-victim story, 42–43, 44–45. *See also* Hero; Offender; Trickster; Victim

Christiansen, Tom: urban legend as crime-victim story, 32, 99

Cohen, Daniel: mugging account, 103; murder account, 113

Comedians: urban origin and crime as topic, 13. *See also* Allen, Woody; Humor

Confidence game: urban legend as crime-victim story, 33–34

Connelly, Doris: mugging account, 93–94; murder accounts, 113, 114; rape account, 118

Crime: New York City and oral tradition, xii, xiii; prevalence in America, xiv–xv; prevalance in New York City, 15; American folk tradition, 39; prevalence and crime-victim story, 60; crime-victim story as coping mechanism, 88. *See also* Mugging accounts; Murder accounts; Offender; Rape accounts; Robbery accounts; Victim

Crime prevention: women and techniques, 8–9; mental map and crime-victim story, 62–64; self-defense techniques, 64–65, 67–68; inconspicuous appearance, 65–67; avoidance of enclosed areas, 68–70; cooperation with assailant, 71–72; safety tips and sense of security, 72–73

Crime-victim story: distinguished from crime narrative, xvii; narrative stances, 7; function in urban life, 11–12, 59–60, 61–62, 87–88; recurring themes, 15; first-hand compared to second-hand, 16; narrative subcategories, 16–17; characters, 17–18, 44–45; common settings, 18–19; senseless death, 19–21; suspicion and urban behavior, 21–23; fated victimization, 23–25; bystander apathy, 25–26; trickster, 26–28; clever victim, 28–31; urban legend, 31–38; traditionalization, 40; general characteristics, 40–41; synchronic time, 41–44; suspense, 45–46; narrative asides, 46–48, 53; attention to detail, 49–50; resolutions and codas, 50–51; predictable structure, 51–52; inference, 54; veracity, 54–55; compared to newspaper accounts, 55–59; mental map, 62–64; inconspicuous appearance, 65–67; self-defense, 67–68; avoidance of enclosed areas, 68–70; cooperation with assailant, 71–72; psychological benefits of storytelling, 73–74; humor, 74–75; compared to Goetz case, 78; tourists and New York City, 80; offenders and violence, 81–82; world view of informants, 82–84; racism, 84–86; *just world hypothesis*, 86–87. *See also* Mugging accounts; Murder accounts; Rape accounts; Robbery accounts

Criminal. *See* Offender

Day, Pamela: as informant, 2; narrative on urban character type, 5; mugging accounts, 7–8, 92, 103; crime prevention, 8–9

Death: senseless violence in crime-victim story, 19–21; euphemisms and inference in crime-victim story, 54; acceptance process compared to crime victimization, 73; crime-victim story and popular-culture image of New York City, 80–81. *See also* Murder accounts; Violence

Dialogue: in crime-victim story, 47–48

Diaz, Maria: mugging accounts, 68, 71, 92, 101, 106

Drama: as characteristic of crime-victim story, 40

135